Love to Quilt...

Broderie Perse

The Elegant Quilt

Barbara W. Barber

American Quilter's Society

P. O. Box 3290 • Paducah, KY 42002-3290

Located in Paducah, Kentucky, the American Quilter's Society (AQS), is dedicated to promoting the accomplishments of today's quilters. Through its publications and events, AQS strives to honor today's quiltmakers and their work – and inspire future creativity and innovation in quiltmaking.

EXECUTIVE EDITOR: JANE R. MC CAULEY
CONTRIBUTING EDITOR: MARY JO KURTEN
BOOK DESIGN & ILLUSTRATIONS: WHITNEY HOPKINS
COVER: KAREN CHILES
TECHNICAL EDITOR: HELEN SQUIRE
PHOTOGRAPHY: CHARLEY LYNCH

Library of Congress Cataloging-in-Publication Data

Barber, Barbara (Barbara W.)
    Broderie perse : the elegant quilt / Barbara Barber.
        p. cm. -- (Love to quilt)
    Includes bibliographical references (p.)
    ISBN 0-89145-875-1
    1. Appliqué--Patterns. 2. Quilting--Patterns. 3. Trapunto.
4. Quilts. 5. Cnintz. I. Title. II Series.
TT779.B37 1996
746.46'041--dc21   96-49791
                                        CIP

Additional copies of this book may be ordered from: American Quilter's Society, P.O. Box 3290, Paducah, KY 42002-3290 @ $14.95. Add $2.00 for postage & handling.

Printed in the U.S.A. by Image Graphics, Paducah, KY

Contents

Preface

When I first looked at antique chintz quilts, it was only with admiration.

The Shelburne Museum in Shelburne, Vermont, has in its collection a substantial array of antique chintz and/or broderie perse quilts.

It was by happenstance that I viewed some of this collection on display at the Vermont Quilt Festival, Northfield, Vermont. Immediately I was drawn to them, scrutinizing carefully their method of construction, all the while admiring their enduring beauty.

Chintz, as a fabric, came to colonial America first from the mother country, England. Of course, it was not English in origin, but was printed in either India or Egypt, both localities being involved in the production of printed cotton fabrics.

The technique of cutting individual design elements from the printed chintzes to disperse and appliqué onto a less expensive base fabric (broderie perse) arose out of the scarcity and expense of early chintzes. Broderie perse, a French word meaning Persian embroidery, facilitated the creation of a bed covering with an opulent look, but at an affordable cost.

Eventually my admiration grew to a more formal interest and gave way to curiosity about the actual construction. Once I passed over the line from admiration to actually entertaining the idea of producing a broderie perse quilt myself, I began to look with "new eyes." Once I made the decision to proceed with a quilt of my own in the broderie perse, chintz framework, I was faced with a multitude of questions and forced to make new decisions each step of the way.

Just as I found satisfying responses to these questions, mostly by trial and error, so this publication will address these issues so someone new to this technique may follow a somewhat less tedious path, but with equally rewarding results.

Barbara W. Barber

Introduction

*M*uch of the chintz imported into or manufactured in the United States in the late eighteenth and nineteenth centuries was used for clothing, draperies, and for furniture covering. But some of the more appealing chintz was reserved for the making of quilts.

The Shelburne Museum in Shelburne, Vermont, has some of the loveliest of these pieces in their extensive quilt collection.

For inspiration, history, and comments, I have included pictures of three quilts from that collection.

IF I WERE BEGINNING AGAIN

Making a large quilt for the first broderie perse project is a full-blown example of "Fools rush in where angels fear to tread."

My advice to anyone interested in this fascinating technique, as it is to students when I teach broderie perse appliqué, is to "start small."

In class, I provide a kit containing an 8" square of unwashed chintz, several chintz cutout motifs, thread for the appliqué, and plenty of instruction. This keeps the project small and within reasonable expectancy of completion. This little piece can be (and has been) adapted into pillows, an elegant evening purse, a framed "picture," and a unique pocket for a vest, T-shirt, or jacket.

By starting small, you won't be overwhelmed, allowing discouragement and frustration to set in. For those who readily take to the process, they have learned the basics; the how and with what, and some advice for going ahead to a larger piece.

Plates 17 and 18 are pictures of small quilts incorporating the broderie perse technique. As you can see, smaller does not mean compromising any of the impact of the chintz appliqué.

One piece (Plate 17) was produced by a talented apprentice, Kitty Kurpiewski, who found herself similarly drawn to the broderie perse technique.

As you can see from these pieces, all broderie perse projects need not be large and involved to be effective. The unique beauty of a chintz appliqué enhances, without regard to the size, shape, and level of difficulty.

Getting Started

CHAPTER ONE

It's seven o'clock in the morning, and I'm heading out. The weather is cool and blustery. I walk into a rural area — part farmland, wooded lots, and a running brook. The trees have turned color — russet, golden, and bronze. Some trees have lost all their leaves, and their bare branches reach to the heavens. How I love to see those dark, naked branches. Their skinny maple arms are outstretched; their fingers point skyward.

Flocks of Canada geese head toward fertile ground that only six weeks ago produced succulent sweet corn. I hear their approach — honks heralding the change of the seasons. Here they come, swooping low, circling about, rising again, a reverse circle above me, one pass over, and, finally, they land. They forage in the fields, green with winter crop. Once again I appreciate their markings given them long ago, at creation, by the Lord's hand. "I thank you and praise you, Lord, for the beauty and strength you created."

I cross over the road so that I may shuffle through the golden maple leaves. Even though the day is overcast, the leaves seem to glow beneath my feet, a reflection of light unseen. Back at home the warmth and aroma of the wood stove greets me; the tea kettle sings. I am ready for that cup of hot tea as the quilt beckons.

WHICH CAME FIRST: THE CHICKEN OR THE EGG?

I think we can all attest to the fact that there are two approaches to making a quilt. First, we have in our possession a "to-die-for fabric" that we want to utilize in a quilt. We mull over the best way to turn that particular fabric into a spectacular quilt. Or, we have in our heads the design for a quilt. Maybe we've seen a special quilt and want to try our hand at the same pattern using our own fabric and interpretation. Perhaps a unique idea pops into mind and to execute it, we must search out applicable fabric.

My chintz quilts have developed through both of these ways. ªUne Belle Mademoiselle" evolved from the first approach. I happened upon a chintz remnant in a barrel of otherwise nondescript fabrics. The color of it caught my eye. The soft blend of roses — printed roses and the color rose — combined with soft green and the spectrum of color between, was what "got me." The old chintz quilts had worked their charm; the desire, the love, the attraction had all worked within simultaneously until my eye was drawn involuntarily to this remnant that challenged me to try my hand on a chintz — in particular, a broderie perse quilt.

My approach was once again to return to the old quilts for design inspiration. "Une Belle" is obviously based on the enduring center diamond geometric format. This would showcase my rose-patterned chintz. My mind ran rampant; quick flashes of my complete quilt ran through my head like scenes in a home movie: a clump of flowers in the larger center; large areas of quilted feathers in the surrounding triangles; wonderful meandering vines burgeoning with opulent roses in the outside border. Quick as a flash these images came to mind as I fingered my newly-found fabric. Are quilters unique in this experience? There's something about the feel of fabric on the fingertip. The smell of all that sizing invigorates my senses, my pulses throb, and my heart gallops along. All my senses are responding to "the call of the fabric." Oh my, such euphoria!

All that slowed me down was the fact that I almost didn't know where or how to begin. I had never made a medallion quilt. I certainly needed border fabric to coordinate with my find; but what did I want, where would I find it and where and how much should I buy? I had never attempted to cut apart designs from any patterns, in other words, broderie perse. I could utilize a branch here, a bud there, and a leaf tucked in somewhere else. But how would I actually appliqué them? What fabric would be suitable for appliquéing my precious fabrics?

"Kensington Garden" and "Tree of Life" were designed using the second approach. I had the design in mind and searched until I found suitable chintz to execute that design. In the case of "Kensington Garden," I wanted clusters of bright, well-proportioned flowers. This design was influenced by Rose Kretsinger's 1946 masterpiece, "Paradise Garden."

Answering all these questions started me on "a road less traveled," but not without signposts; albeit, some very old, though enduring. I was looking back at the antique quilts of the eighteenth and nineteenth century for help and inspiration. At the same time I was forging ahead and making a road of my own in the twentieth century. This book is a result of some of my personal findings. I hope that you, too, will feel the uncontrollable urge to enter "the world of chintz."

CHINTZ

Characteristic of chintz is its glaze. Most of the beautiful chintz/glazed quilts in the museums have never been washed and still have a lovely sheen (almost a patina) after well over a hundred years of existence. Washing often removes this glaze. So it is that I use my chintz fabric unwashed, and I have no intention of washing the completed quilts.

A SIGNIFICANT DIFFERENCE

As you plan the arrangement or placement of the motifs or elements, you'll note that there is a significant difference between traditional appliqué and broderie perse. When you want adjacent corners to look or "read" alike in traditional appliqué, you can achieve this by flipping the template over to produce mirror image elements. You cannot do this with printed motifs. A flower head that is printed facing left must remain that way. So placing the different elements is a challenge. To the observer, all corners are complementary, and opposite corners can be exactly alike. It is a challenge worth the trouble! I love the manipulation of motifs. Yes, I *can* do this. Actually, by arranging and rearranging, clustering and nesting, trial and error, you are manipulating these motifs into a new configuration.

GLOSSARY OF APPLICABLE TERMS

APPLIQUÉ: To sew smaller fabric pieces onto larger ones to create or complete a design.

BASE FABRIC: The background fabric onto which the cutouts are appliquéd.

BINDING: A strip of fabric that frames, finishes, and protects the edge of the quilt.

BORDER, INNER: The fabric frame that surrounds the central portion of a medallion quilt. It can be a strip of whole cloth, patchwork, or a compilation of strips of fabric.

BORDER, OUTER: The fabric frame that surrounds and completes the outside edge of the quilt. Often this fabric is a stripe or pattern that is different from the interior of the quilt. It can be a strip of whole cloth, patchwork, or a compilation of strips of fabric. Bor-

ders must complement all aspects of the quilt.

CORDED BINDING: Cording, encased in a fabric that complements the quilt and binding fabrics, and is placed parallel to the finishing binding.

ELEMENT: A unit or units of design.

MIRROR IMAGE: The reverse reflection that occurs as the result of a 45° miter across identical motifs on a border fabric.

MITER: When two borders are joined with a diagonal seam.

MOTIF: The basic unit of design in the broderie perse sense. Individual pieces that are cut apart or separated from an overlay design on an existing fabric and reassembled in a different design.

MOTIF, BASE: The first motif placed directly on the background fabric in a series of motif appliqué.

MOTIF, OVERLAY: A motif that overlaps a previously positioned motif.

MEDALLION QUILT: A quilt design originating from a central motif that is surrounded by a series of concentric borders.

PANEL: A fabric portion, or length of a quilt top, cut to a predetermined measurement.

SWAG: A circular inner or outer border of a medallion quilt, usually executed in graceful, appliquéd increments to complete a circle or oval.

FABRIC
COLOR

Have you had your colors done? In this process an expert tests your skin tone, eye color, hair shade, etc., and concludes that you are either a Spring, Summer, Autumn, or Winter.

Why do I ask? Because I'm comfortable working with rose, magenta, soft greens, and olive to forest green. It was no surprise to me that when I had my colors done, those that I liked to work with also looked the best on me. Notice "Une Belle" and "Kensington Garden" both fall into that color category. So when making a color choice, why not pick what appeals to you? First, pick a chintz that you really love. Then, picking up the colors from that fabric, select coordinating and accent fabrics. The narrow strips of solid fabrics incorporated into "Une Belle's" borders helped define the perimeters without overwhelming the design.

Deep magenta and forest green picked up the printed flower colors of the chintz for "Kensington Garden." Using those bold solids in the swag balanced the round inner border, giving definition to the circular layout of flowers. The two fabrics in the covered cording and binding framed the piece without overpowering it.

So what is it we expect color to do for us?
- Define our preferences.
- Coordinate the design.
- Coordinate the colors in the overall design.
- Accent the soft edge of an inner border.
- Showcase the quilting ("Kensington Garden" swag).
- Frame the whole quilt ("Tree of Life," in particular).
- Give us pleasure.

WHERE TO SHOP

- Tear yourself away from quilt fabrics, at least for this project. Wander into the drapery department or even a furniture store or a decorator's establishment. Yes, there is a life outside of quilt fabric. Hard to believe, isn't it?
- Read the labels; it's 100% cotton that you are looking for.
- Do not pick soft, pliable fabric for motifs; it ravels as you appliqué. Look for chintz. It will be on the stiff side with a noticeable glaze.
- Don't overlook the remnant barrel; that's where I found the motif fabric for "Une Belle."
- Combining several fabrics can be interesting; flowers from one, a bird from another, maybe a butterfly from yet another. But keep scale and appropriate color in mind.

MOTIFS

Motifs are the basic units of a printed fabric that can be cut apart. Look especially for flowers printed singly so 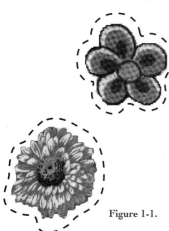 you can cut them out. Leave a good seam allowance of background fabric around each one (Fig 1-1). For the appliquéd motifs, I always use 100% cotton chintz. It has a high thread count that keeps it from raveling excessively. This is a major consideration since the blanket stitch is done over the raw edge and not turned under as in traditional appliqué.

Figure 1-1.

I look for a well defined, precise edge in the motif. It cannot be fuzzy or have a soft look. It should also lend itself to being cut apart — i.e., have a distinctive shape. You will want to use single flowers somewhere in your design, so pick a fabric conducive to this. The design is usually dictated by the fabric. Don't be reluctant to combine various chintz pieces: flowers from one fabric, butterflies from another, birds from yet another. Notice the background color and design of the chintz. Unusual colors and shades or designs within the background should be avoided. It is too hard to match the background fabric to which it will be appliquéd.

There are times when a portion of the background surrounding the motif must be included in the cutout appliqué. Any printing on this fabric and not on the overall base background fabric will immediately draw the eye. So avoid any stripes, fleur-de-lis, or distracting details. The objective of broderie perse is to assimilate a variety of motifs on a new background or base fabric and make it appear as natural on that background as if it had been printed that way.

BACKGROUND

The backgrounds of the motif fabrics and the background to which the motifs will be appliquéd must be as close a match as possible. The easiest colors or shades to match are white and off-white to the beige shades. To my eye, the bone to beige shades lend a rich patina to an opulent technique. "Une Belle Mademoiselle's" background is Jeff Guetcheon polished cotton. This is a good choice, for several reasons:
- It is available in a multitude of colors and shades.
- It is easy to needle.
- It has an attractive glaze.
- It cost less than the 100% cotton chintz — a practical consideration for any project.

This fabric would also be a good choice for touches of coordinating or accent color to be incorporated into border designs. Now, this said, I must admit "Kensington Garden" and "Tree of Life" both have chintz backgrounds. I just couldn't resist its crisp, glazed, traditional feel.

BORDERS

Borders, as you well know, can make or break a quilt! Drapery fabric comes with a color strip along the selvage. Clip it and carry it everywhere. You never know when you'll come upon what may be your perfect border. A quick comparison between your prospective border and your color-matching strip is imperative. If the colors are not just right, ask if other colors are available. Design and scale, of course, are prime considerations; the border must complement the motifs.

When I chose the border print for "Une Belle Mademoiselle," I was not fully aware of all that I was doing, but:
- The colors were right.
- The print included features that reflected the motif — roses, in this case.
- It "felt" right, sort of like making pie crust or kneading bread; the "feel" was important to me.

"Une Belle Mademoiselle's" border fabric is not chintz. It is a very soft drapery fabric that ravels easily. After a considerable search, it met my other requirements. It also revealed the fact that no elaborate hand quilting will ever show in this kind of fabric; it simply disappears "down-in." That's okay. I was tired of fancy quilting by the time I got to the borders anyway!

The "Tree of Life" border was picked by my good friend and fellow quilter, Rose Koretski. The center construction of the tree was well underway when we foraged forth into the fabric stores in search of just the right fabrics. With the "Tree" panel in hand, we truly commandeered the drapery department. Picking out numerous possibilities, we mounted the "Tree" panel on bolts of fabric, displayed border candidates alongside, eliminated, and retained possibilities. Rose made the final decision when a beautiful paisley was put alongside. All the colors were complementary, the designs were certainly compatible, but neither of us were clever enough to realize its one drawback; one-way paisley. Oh, what fun that was to miter! We'll discuss this obstacle further in the "Tree of Life" chapter. So a word to the wise: look at fabric with mitering possibilities or impossibilities in mind.

BACKING

I have three primary concerns when I select backing fabric. I want it to be complementary in color to the quilt top. I hope for needling ease. And I like a match with quilting thread color.

COMPLEMENT TO THE QUILT TOP

You are creating a rich quilt, with sophistication in pattern and color, so carry that look to the back. Think of backing fabric as an extension of the front. You have made the top with great care and detail, so select backing fabric that will complement that beauty and rich-

ness. Consider that when the quilt is complete. A flowery or a deep-colored backing fabric might cast its influence on the front, causing it to look off-color or diluted.

NEEDLE EASE

"Une Belle Mademoiselle's" backing included a touch of polyester, definitely not conducive to easy quilting. The day I set my quilting needle to it should have been the day I removed all the basting and the backing and purchased 100% cotton instead! But no, I didn't want to waste a day; so I spent another 538 hours over five months wishing I had.

Two years later, when I made "Kensington Garden", I was not much wiser. I used the same unwashed 100% cotton chintz fabric for the backing that I used for the background of the top. Hand quilting that quilt was like doing penance — like quilting through two cookie sheets. I promised myself I'd never do that to myself again, and I've kept that promise. I'm so good to me!

I'm both older and wiser. The background of the "Tree of Life" top is unwashed 100% cotton chintz. The backing is a very soft fabric with a design that gives a tea-dyed look. It was a joy to quilt, and it has been washed, washed, and washed.

PREPARATION

A dark backing and light thread will look lovely if your stitches are perfect. But it's easier on you, the quilter, if you select thread the same color as the quilt back. All my 100% cotton chintz is used unwashed. Despite the manufacturers' assurances of glaze retention after washing, I have found that it dissipates or disappears altogether. Antique chintz quilts were usually unwashed. So, who am I to argue with their success? I even used the Guetcheon polished cotton unwashed for the background, borders, and binding. For needling ease, I did prewash the backing.

THE LAST SHALL BE FIRST

Because the borders are an integral element of the medallion quilt design, I will address their selection and use prior to the making of the quilt body. Instead of making the borders fit the quilt, I do just the opposite in a medallion quilt. I am contemplating border fabric selection as it relates to the prospective quilt body, selecting an appropriate element to miter, and the where and how of mitering as it impacts the amount of fabric purchased.

BORDERS AND CORNERS

The quilts in this book incorporate printed fabric into their borders. "Une Belle Mademoiselle's" inner border has printed stripes. Its outer border has printed stripes with a printed floral design. "Tree of Life" has a printed floral border with a paisley design. Whatever border print you choose, the treatment of the corners will be the focal point. All corners must match or be identical to be symmetrical. Identical corners produce a continuous, unbroken appearance. The design flows gracefully around the border with no interruption. Just how is this continuous appearance achieved in a border? The mitering must be accurately done.

Figure 1-2.

What exactly is a miter? A miter is a joint made with two pieces of fabric whose joined ends have been cut at equal angles. Usually, and in these quilts, the angle is 45°. The border fabrics meet in a diagonal seam, or miter; a miter corner looks just like the corner of a picture frame (Fig. 1-2).

Plate 1. *Detail of one of "Une Belle's" corners on outer and inner borders reflecting the mirror-image miter achieved by the diagonal cut passing through the same pink flower.*

WHERE TO MITER

On each complete border, every corner should be identical. In addition, every corner should be a mirror image joint, or miter (Plate 1).

Also note the narrow inserts of color bordering the large outer border print.

To achieve a mirror image, each end of the cut borders must pass through the same design element and at the same point in the element.

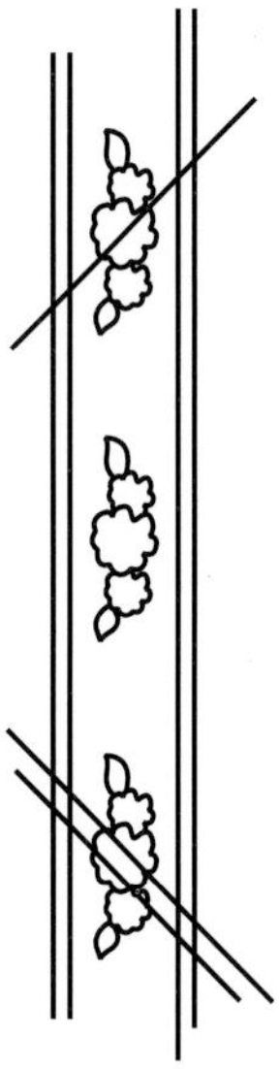

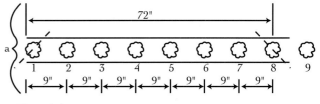

Figure 1-3.

Select a predominant element within the border print, as in Plate 1. I selected the pink flower.

To produce the mirror image, a 45° line must be drawn through this element at exactly the same point – *both ends of the border* (Fig. 1-3).

As these pieces are joined, or mitered, the mirror image magic will result.

1. Study your border fabric.
2. Select an element for a 45° miter.
3. Add seam allowances.
4. Account for repeat in the fabric.

Miter requirements and repeats in border fabric go hand-in-hand; one completely influences the other.

Repeats also influence the size of the quilt. Consider this scenario: You have found just the right border fabric for use as outer and inner borders by following the above steps. The selected element for potential miter repeats every 9". Therefore, based on 9" increments (miter placements), you can now determine the final size of the completed quilt by the length you cut the outer border. In our scenario, based on the 9" repeat, the size of the quilt will change by 9", depending on which of the element repeats that is selected.

72"

a

1   2   3   4   5   6   7   8   9

9"   9"   9"   9"   9"   9"   9"

Figure 1-4.

Executing the mirror-image miter at element #8 (Fig. 1-4) will produce an outside length of 9" x 7 increments, or 63". To increase the length of the piece, proceed to element #9 (Fig. 1-5), and the size will increase by 9", or a total of 72". All of these factors will determine the length of each successive border and, in turn,

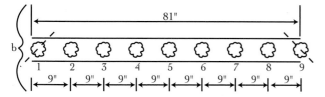

Figure 1-5.

the size of the finished quilt. All of this will have a direct influence on the estimate of the required fabric.

Figure how long the outside border will be between selected mitering and continue to move inward. The dimensions of the inner borders are determined by the same method. Review steps 1 – 4 on page 9.

The method to determine the required width of fabric between the inner and outer borders (Fig. 1-6) is developed further in the chapter Designing a Medallion Quilt.

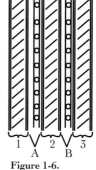

Figure 1-6.
Outer borders 1, 2, 3 – three per width.
Inner borders A and B – two per width.

Figure 1-7.
Border fabric that "reads" the same from left to right (symmetrical).

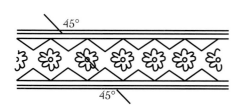

Figure 1-8.
A miter angle that can "feed" on itself.

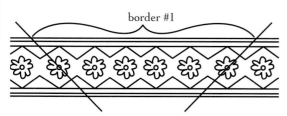

Figure 1-9.
Border fabrics that read the same from left or right allow consecutive mitered pieces to be cut with no waste.

Figure 1-10.
Border fabric with one-way print (asymmetrical).

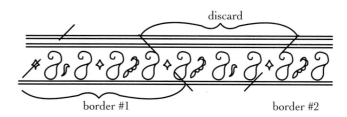

Figure 1-11.
Miter placement on asymmetrical border design.

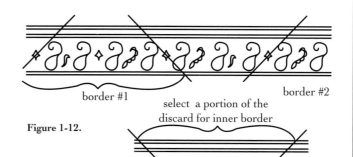

Figure 1-12.

HOW TO MITER

•The Omni Grid® 45/90° triangle is just the tool to help you execute a proper miter. Align the bottom side of the triangle on a sheet of your border print (Fig. 1-13).

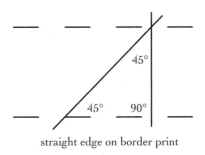

straight edge on border print

Figure 1-13.

•With the diagonal passing precisely through the selected motif, mark that diagonal with a sharp marking pencil.

•The straight edges of the border print set the parameters of the border width. Mark them on the wrong side of the fabric if the print itself is not clear enough to be used as a stitching line. These drawn lines are all stitching lines and require seam allowances.

•The diagonal produces a perfect 45° line. Repeat the same exercise but in the opposite direction at the other end of the border. You have set up for a proper miter resulting in a mirror image that makes the border flow (Fig. 1-14).

mirror image miter

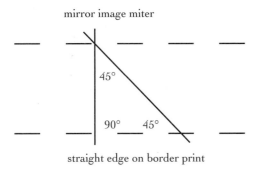

straight edge on border print

Figure 1-14.

Remember: The drawn line is the sewing line. Seam allowances must be added. Note that when stitching mitered borders to your quilt, stitch only on the stitching line. Never pass over into the seam allowance so that your borders will lay flat and even.

FABRIC ESTIMATING

The amount of border fabric needed depends on the border style, the border repeat, the number of borders printed per width of fabric, and the ultimate quilt size (determined by border repeat). Depending on how many borders you figured per length, purchase enough for your individual design. My general rule of thumb for motifs is three yards. This usually yields enough flowers, trunks, stems, etc., for experimenting. In some cases, the design may have to be altered slightly, but that holds true no matter how much fabric you buy! So limit yourself to three yards. For backing, two to three lengths of fabric, each as long as the quilt, should be enough, depending upon fabric width.

CHAPTER TWO

*B*y definition a medallion quilt has a central motif that is surrounded by a series of concentric borders. In this chapter, I will explain how to determine the dimensions of the medallion quilt: center, outside border, inset, and inner border.

"Une Belle Mademoiselle" is a square quilt, as are many medallion quilts. Often the width and the height are identical. The following calculations to determine quilt size are based on this assumption. One might reasonably assume that the center would be a likely starting point for determining the basic dimensional characteristics of a medallion quilt. But the center dimensions can be varied. I will show that both the outside border and the inside border, because of the importance of the miters involved, actually define a quilt's dimensions. They must be assigned a higher priority.

OUTSIDE BORDER

As you work with the following data, it will become increasingly apparent that the width of the outside border and the selection of the miter locations (repeats) within the chosen fabric will be the most instrumental in determining many of the quilt dimensions.

Look again at Plate 1, page 10.

•If you have selected a similar floral border print, ascertain where your miter can properly be positioned. Then determine the pattern repeat within the border fabric. The formation of a 45° cut at the dissection points selected will define the outside dimension of the overall quilt.

•Visualize the four corners of your outside borders, the miters of which are all pointing to the exact center of your completed quilt. It might be helpful to get a piece of graph paper with a ¼ " grid, to help keep you on track (Fig. 2-1).

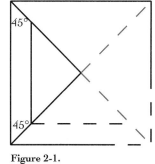

Figure 2-1.

•Determine your miter placement as detailed in Chapter 3. Select an element to dissect and use for corner miters.

•On the wrong side of your fabric, use a plastic see-through ruler with 45° angle marks. With the angle on the border's side, line up the ruler through the center of your design and draw with a sharp pencil the 45° angle. This is the sewing line. Extend the marking line so the intersecting point is well established.

•As you determine the outside border's width and length, sketch this information on your graph paper. Note that the border's position becomes fixed; there is only one location on your grid that will properly project the mitered ends of the border to the precise center of the quilt your are creating.

INNER BORDER

•The inner border must fit within the parameters established by the outside border. Using the same process as you used for the outside border, determine the length of the inner border. Find the best location options for the miter within the border fabric and determine the fabric's repeat. The 45° miter locations must fall along the same lines as projected by the outside border miters; however, the location as radiated from the center of the quilt can be varied to accommodate this requirement.

•The width of each of these borders is more an artistic than a geometric concern, since the spaces between the two borders (inset) may be filled using a variety of options.

•Now add this information to your grid. Note that the all of the quilt's major dimensions have now been defined by this process —center, both borders, and the inset (Fig. 2-2).

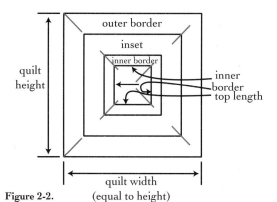

Figure 2-2.

INSET

The inset is the space remaining between the two borders. Its dimensions must equate to the borders already defined. Thus all of the inset's dimensions can be calculated and scaled as a check from your grid (if you drew it accurately) as follows:

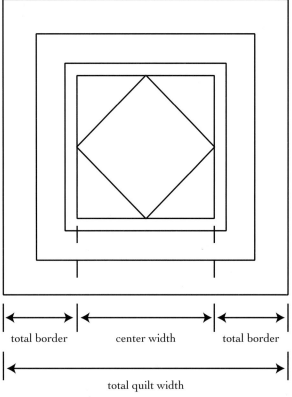

Figure 2-3

Total Quilt Width = Center Width + 2 "Total" Borders
Total Quilt Height = Center Height + 2 "Total" Borders
Total Border = Outer Border + Inner Border + Inset

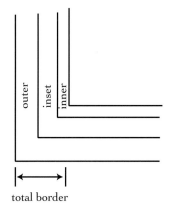

Figure 2-4.

To obtain the width of the inset:

• Determine the length of the outer border (to miter tip or quilt dimension).

• Determine the length of the inner border (to the miter tip).

• Subtract the second from the first. This represents two insets and two outer border widths.

• Multiply the outside border width by two. Subtract this from the above. This figure represents the width of two insets.

• Divide the above dimension in two. This is the width of a single inset.

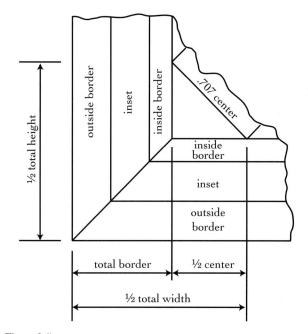

Figure 2-5.

Example: (Based on the chapter 1 scenario for a 9" floral repeat)
   Length of outer border to miter tip: 72" (9" x 8")
   Length of inner border to miter tip: 36" (9" x 4")
   The difference is 36". This represents two insets and two outside border widths.
   Assume a 7" outside border width.
   Multiplying the 7" outer border by two produces 14".
   Subtract 14" from 36" = 22".

Divide 22" by two for a single inset width of 11".

Assuming a 4" inner border width will define a 28" center.

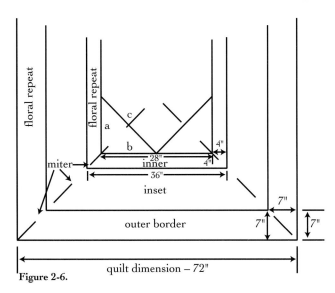

Figure 2-6.

CENTER SQUARE AND TRIANGLES

The dimensions relating to the center square and the resulting triangles can be calculated using the gemoetry you may have forgotten from your high school days.

Since the center medallion square is placed at a 45° angle to the sides of the quilt, it will relate to the center measurement as indicated (Fig. 2-3).

A TRIGONOMETRIC REVIEW:

Quilters *always* work with *right* triangles. At least that is almost always the intent. A right triangle has one 90° angle. This makes the overall quilt square or rectangular. There are trigonometric laws that apply, providing consistent, if not simple, methods of determining the quilt's various dimensions. This is especially true for the diagonals. All you have to do is remember your high school trig. (Oh, this is why we had to sit through all that boring stuff we knew we would never use!) The hypotenuse (the longest side) of any

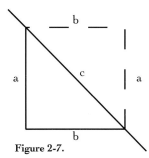

Figure 2-7.

right triangle (Fig. 2-7) relates to the other two sides per the following formula:

$$C^2 = a^2 + b^2$$

And for squares, a = b; so $C^2 = 2 a^2$ and C = a x 1.414.

And 1.414 enters the scene. That number happens to be the square root of two. For "Une Belle," the center midpoint of the square medallion has a diagonal projecting from points at its center of .707 (½ of 1.414) times the full center width.

COMPLETING THE EXAMPLE IDENTIFIED ABOVE:

For a 28" center, each side of the center square will be 0.707 x 28", or 19.8" or, using the above formula directly, a = 14, or half the center square: $14^2 = 196$; 196 + 196 = 392; $C^2 = 392$; C = 19.8".

Now you have the size of every element. I mark on the reverse side of fabric. The drawn line is, once again, the stitching line. Be sure to add seam allowances before cutting.

PLANNING THE QUILT

A precise drawing of all of the elements, aided by grid paper, enhances the quilt planning and verifies the calculations. Hopefully you have discovered this. Now transfer these measurements to fabric. *Do not deviate!* These are the exact measurements. Make allowances for the seams. Include in your drawing, as illustrated, the 90° angles drawn for miters; they will help you to achieve proper measurements (Fig. 2-8).

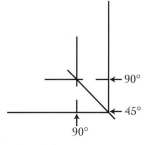

Figure 2-8.

•Mark the large triangles with the sides of the right angles on the straight grain of the fabric (Fig. 2-9).

•After marking the appropriate sewing line on the background fabric, cut out

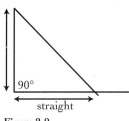

Figure 2-9.

leaving a ½" seam allowance. Staystitch in the allowance. Stitch the bias sections very carefully. The appliqué requires much handling of the background pieces, so a stitch in time.

"UNE BELLE MADEMOISELLE"

I have described the "how" of planning "Une Belle's " format, but it is the actual use of the chintz that makes the spirit sing. We quilters are pulled in by the appeal of "that special fabric," as I have already noted. So this chapter addresses the broderie perse portion of "Une Belle."

My remnant limited me to exactly what I had in hand, about 1½ yards of fabulous chintz. Using one large clump of roses together, I set about appliquéing it to the background square. I didn't really know what I was doing. Setting the clump on point looked best, so I proceeded. Eventually I added several more roses and leaves to this clump to even it out. I kept the large leaves toward the bottom of the clump to anchor it visually (Plate 2). Later, I located suitable border fabric. Thanks to my husband's knowledge of mathematics, and trial and error, we figured out the necessary length and width of the broderie perse inset.

Plate 3. *"Une Belle Mademoiselle," bottom border detail.*

appliquéd over the area after I had seamed it (Plate 4). Then I assembled the quilt top (center, triangles, borders, outside borders, and inset) once the appliqué was complete — except for the yet-to-be mitered inset cor-

Plate 4 *"Une Belle Mademoiselle," corner detail.*

Plate 2. *"Une Belle Mademoiselle," center block detail.*

I carefully cut my fabric. Next my task was to fill the inset with appliquéd roses, vines, buds, and leaves meandering asymmetrically around the quilt (Plate 3). I was relieved to discover that as I used the last of my vines, the border was filled. Whew!

Where the corners were joined, I used a motif

ners. These motifs were appliquéd after the inset miters were pieced, pleasingly covering the mitered seam. I basted the quilt and began to quilt. I knew I wanted it to look spectacular.

On a remnant of fabric, I experimented with several designs for background quilting. The stipple looked best. Asking a friend for her advice and choice, she said, "I like the stipple best, but Barbara, if you did nothing but quilt 24 hours a day for a year, you would never complete the quilt." That was just the challenge I needed! The quilting was completed in five months. Within the printed borders, I followed the stripe. The very narrow strips of accent fabric

First row

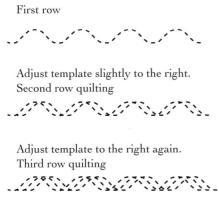

Adjust template slightly to the right.
Second row quilting

Adjust template to the right again.
Third row quilting

Figure 2-10.

incorporated into the borders are simply but effectively quilted (Fig. 2-10).

I was working on "Une Belle" in 1986 when the *Challenger* exploded at Cape Canaveral. "Une Belle" knew my surging pride as I watched the *Challenger* soar. It felt my shock and despair when I witnessed it explode, taking with it the lives of seven astronauts and the hopes and dreams of all America. My quilt felt my tears that fell, wetting its fabric and flowers. It knew my grief and sympathy, my prayers and love for the family and friends that were personally involved in the tragedy. It knew my faith that though their bodies were destroyed, their spirits would still live. My quilt was my therapy, my security in an ever-changing, unsettling world. My stitches blurred yet progressed in the tapestry of life. I tremble sometimes when I remember what that quilt knows about me.

Plate 5. *"Kensington Garden," detail.*

HOW DID "MY *KENSINGTON GARDEN*" GROW?

The making of "Une Belle" whetted my appetite. I felt that I had answered many of my original questions pertaining to this technique called broderie perse. Without further delay, I jumped into the planning and construction of "Kensington Garden" (Plate 19, page 33). Optically, this is a medallion quilt. It is derived from Rose Kretsinger's "Paradise Garden." This quilt literally grew from a seed of an idea to a garden in full bloom.

PLANNING MOTIF PLACEMENT

To get the desired size for "Kensington," I used a full center panel with two half panels on either side. The handwork was done on the individual panels before they were joined. It is much easier to work on smaller pieces than the entire quilt top (Fig. 2-11). Naturally, much planning was involved. I basted the pieces of background fabric together and planned the motif placement. This included basting the chintz elements in place, leaving the loose few that would eventually be appliquéd where the panels joined. Then I proceeded with placing all the elements until I was pleased with the results.

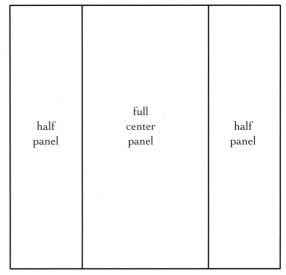

| half panel | full center panel | half panel |

Figure 2-11.

SWAG PLACEMENT

The swag template and placement were determined while the panels were basted by adapting the Jinny Beyer "folded paper" method. The swag is based on a full circle design divided into wedge-shaped divisions on the circle. Due to the large size of the circle I was working with, I began with a quadrant of paper, or ¼ of the circle. I found and marked with a pin or a loop of double thread (Fig. 2-12) the very center of the quilt, the centers of each side, and the centers of the top and

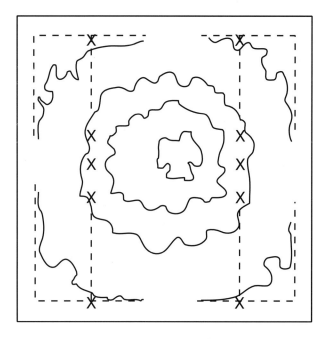

X's mark flopping motifs

Figure 2-12.

the bottom. The radius, or side of my quadrant, was the distance from the center to the outside edge of the prospective swag (Fig. 2-13).

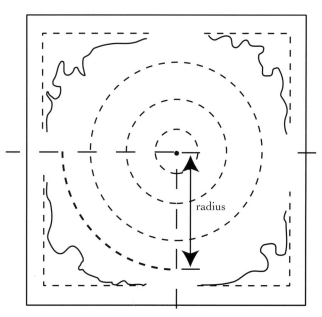

radius

Figure 2-13.

To draft a circular arc, I used compass points on my yardstick. These commercially available attachments are an easy way to make a large compass. I cut the paper on this arc line, giving me a true quadrant (Fig. 2-14). To divide the quadrant into a usable wedge, I folded the paper in half once (Fig. 2-15), then again (Fig. 2-16), to produce an accurate wedge, It measured ¼ of the quadrant, or 1⁄16 of the complete circle. In other words, I made 16 swag units to exactly fit the full circle.

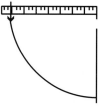

Figure 2-14.

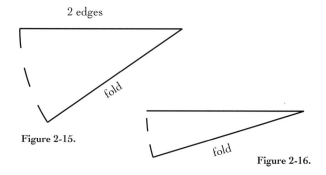

2 edges

fold

Figure 2-15.

fold

Figure 2-16.

Cutting through multiple layers of paper causes inaccuracies. Instead I used the last folded segment as a guide. I duplicated it perfectly on additional paper. Once this pattern was drafted, I scalloped the outer edge of the swag using a plate as a pattern. I cut off and discarded the excess (Fig. 2-17). Then I gently sloped the inside of the swag by using an even larger plate for the drawn line delineation (Fig. 2-18).

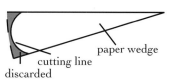

paper wedge

cutting line

discarded

Figure 2-17.

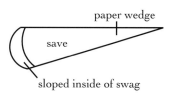

paper wedge

save

sloped inside of swag

Figure 2-18.

I cut off the swag on the drawn line and saved the paper wedge. This produced a swag pattern that perfectly fit the desired place on my "Kensington Garden."

Okay, so far, so good. Next I needed to mark the basted panels of my quilt top with the *exact* placement of the planned swag. Using the saved portion of the wedge pattern as a large template, I planned my swag placement. Unfolding the previously folded paper quadrant, I aligned the edges of my single paper wedge with the edges and folds of the quilt quadrant.

Then I drew around the scallop (Fig. 2-19). Repeating this four times and marking each folded wedge produced the

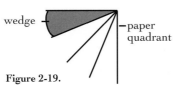

Figure 2-19.

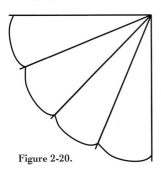

Figure 2-20.

necessary scalloped markings. I trimmed and discarded the excess below the scalloped edge of the paper (Fig. 2-20). Using the previously marked center of the quilt plus the centers of the sides, top, and bottom, I carefully placed and aligned perfectly the new paper template on the basted top. I always kept the point of the template on the center mark and the radius of the paper quadrant aligned with the perimeter marks.

I marked each scallop/swag joint first with temporary pins, then with looped doubled thread (Fig. 2-21). I repeated this for three more quadrants to make a total of 16 swags, a full circle. At this stage of the game I had three panels basted together

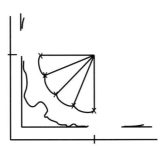

Figure 2-21.

Figure 2-22.

with the layout of motifs basted in place, except for those flopping over the panel seams (Fig. 2-22). I had sewn threads to mark swag placement, and I had a pattern for my swag (Fig. 2-23).

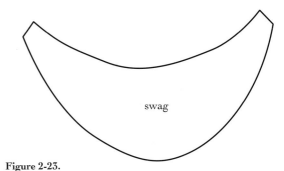

swag

Figure 2-23.

Swag Construction

I wanted to have a two-color swag, so I divided my swag pattern, keeping the top part a bit wider (Fig. 2-24).

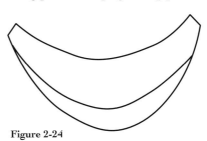

Figure 2-24

All the cut edges of my pattern are sewing lines; seam allowances must be added. For ease of handling, I removed the basting stitches joining the three background panels (Fig. 2-25). Next I blanket stitched all the chintz cutout motifs on the separate, background panels. Finally, these background panels were

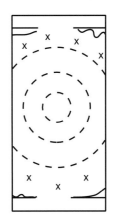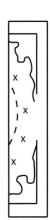

Figure 2-25.

reassembled (stitched together) and the flopping motifs over the seams were blanket stitched into place. Confidently using my swag pattern, I forged ahead.

The top, fuller part of the swag was cut out of deep magenta 100% cotton, unwashed chintz and carefully appliquéd to the narrow, bottom section of the swag. It was made of the same material and content, but it was forest green (Fig. 2-26). Both of these colors accent the flowers and foliage in the chintz cutouts.

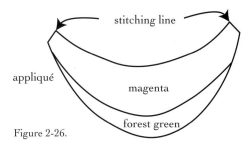

Figure 2-26.

Figure 2-27.

After making my quota of 16 swags, I joined them into a full circle, each connected to the other by just a few running stitches. I had a full circle of swags (Fig. 2-27).

I assembled the swag and placed it on the joined background panels. What a day of rejoicing it was when my swag circle (three stitches held swag to swag) actually fit and lay perfectly, each point finding its own tailor tack!

I appliquéd the full circle in place to complete the top construction — five months working time and counting (Fig. 2-28).

Figure 2-28.

QUILTING DESIGN

Thinking the motif fabric depicted grapes, I designed a quilting pattern that placed a bunch of grapes within each appliquéd swag (Plate 6). Eventual-

Plate 6. *"Kensington Garden," detail.*

ly, I realized that my fabric portrayed gooseberries, not grapes (Plate 7). But the grapes, already quilted, were retained. Please note that this was an adaptable stencil; it has actually been used to festoon the borders of the living room walls of several homes.

Plate 7. *"Kensington Garden," detail.*

ONE FLEW OVER THE QUILTER'S NEST

As work on a quilt progresses, I am usually neat and tidy, placing the threads and clippings into the proper receptacle. But as the quilt nears completion, impatience sets in; I am no longer neat, and debris falls where it may — surrounding my work space.

When "Kensington Garden" was completed, even as I crawled on my hands and knees collecting the debris, it occurred to me: "What a tidy nest this would be — for posterity." Thus, "One Flew Over the Quilter's Nest" was born. This creation includes basting thread, masking tape, empty spools, and a broken needle threader. It is complete with a hand-hooked, color coordinated rug base.

DEVELOPING THE ELEMENTS

So far, we have done a great deal of head work, establishing the exact measurements of the integrating parts. That's enough plotting and planning. I know that you are ready to get underway. So break out the sewing pouch, locate your Ginghers, and we will get on with the actual, hands-on construction.

WORKING SUPPLIES

You will need a basic sewing kit, including small, sharp embroidery scissors such as those made by Gingher, number 10-12 quilting needles, and dressmaker's weight basting thread to match the background fabric.

THREAD SELECTION

When making "Une Belle," I started the blanket stitches using quilting thread. I thought this made sense, since I was using unwashed fabric and dressmaker's thread would probably fray. However, the quilting thread did not produce a neat and tidy knot. It was too waxed, I suppose. Next I tried waxing dressmaker's thread to strengthen it. That kept it from looking as neat as I had expected. Finally, I did all the appliqué with polyester-covered cotton thread. It wore out quickly, so I used short, 8" lengths. It took ten minutes to work that length and produced approximately 1" of blanket stitch. (And the piece got to looking pretty messy on the back with all the thread ends dangling.)

By the time the construction of "Kensington Garden" was underway, I had found DMC 100% cotton machine embroidery thread #50. It is stronger than dressmaker's thread, so I can work with a longer piece.

The spools hold a number of yards, and the thread has a nice sheen. It comes in many colors and shades. It was difficult to find a supplier in my area, however. Here are two sources:

DMC Corporation
107 Trumball Street
Elizabeth, NJ 07206
(908) 351-4550

Herrschners
2800 Hoover Road
Stevens Point, WI 54492
1-800-411-0838

CUTTING OUT MOTIFS

Rough cut the motifs using the sharp embroidery scissors. Leave ¼" to ⅛" background material all around. Accuracy is not important at this time. Just cut by eye. Either include as part of a whole motif or disregard the small, feathery portions of the design too detailed to cut. If they are important to the design, they can be executed later in embroidery or by permanent pen drawing.

Include lengths of vine with some clusters if that is pertinent to your design. If you are fortunate enough to have sizable clusters of several flowers, fruit, feathers, birds, etc., try to utilize them as complete units rather than cutting them apart. Look at the close-up of "Kensington Garden's" corner (Plate 8). A large cluster of several flowers was appliquéd as a whole motif. Eventually, several leaves and an additional flower motif

Plate 8. *"Kensington Garden," detail.*

motif were added to the basic large cluster. This large motif covers the corner miter of the inset.

ARRANGING APPLIQUÉ ELEMENTS

A good rule of thumb is to arrange the motifs as nature presents them. Nature is more curved than straight. Also, buds, leaves, and blossoms usually stem from a single source, even if it is not entirely visible. Partial elements can be inserted in back of the complete motifs. Never discard even the smallest leaf; you never know when it will be just the right thing.

Corners are conducive to clustering. Use the heaviest part of the design in them.

Arrange bits and pieces of vines to give a continuous effect. Where the ends of the vines meet, cluster a flower or two to cover the seam.

BASTING

Once the planning is done, then comes the basting. I have found no quick way to achieve this, so just plunge in. Each element must be well basted into place. Absolutely no glitch! A glitch is an errant tuck or pleat. Once a glitch, always a glitch, so be forewarned!

Lay the background piece flat, elements in place (absolutely flat as well). As inconvenient as it is, I always baste directly on the table, smoothing as I go along. Baste within the motif, from the center out, and also about ¼" inside the printed area. This eliminates having the basting stitches that interfere with the actual cutting and/or appliqué (Fig. 2-29).

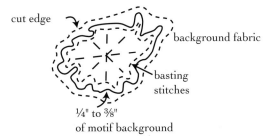

Figure 2-29.
Baste ¼" from the printed edge and within the motif from the center out.

WHAT WHEN OVERLAP CUT AWAY

Position all key elements. If you are adding additional pieces — leaves, birds, vines, tree trunks, branches — tuck the surrounding ones sufficiently under so that the application of the new pieces will completely cover the raw edge of the tucked piece. Cut away the material tucked under, leaving only ¼" or so overlap. Just don't do it prematurely! I don't cut away until I am actually

basting in place (Fig. 2-30).

The opposite is also true. Neighboring elements, if not superimposed on one another, should be well separated so the blanket stitch does not interfere side-by-side. I avoid stitches upon stitches. It just looks too clumsy (Fig. 2-31).

Figure 2-30.

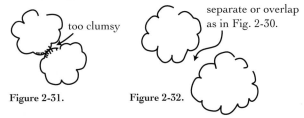

Figure 2-31. **Figure 2-32.**

METHODS AND APPLIQUÉING

Is every motif well basted? Are all arrangements to your liking? Then we are ready for the actual appliqué! There are various methods of appliqué. We will discuss traditional, blanket stitch, and the buttonhole stitch. No matter what method is preferred, all begin and end with a knot on the back or wrong side of the background fabric.

TRADITIONAL APPLIQUÉ

In traditional appliqué the edge of the printed design on the fabric motif is the seam line, and the raw edge of the fabric surrounding the design must be turned under. It can be turned under with the point of the needle as the work progresses (Fig. 2-33).

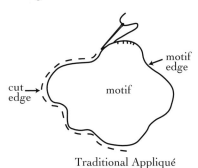

Traditional Appliqué

Figure 2-33.

Clip curves to the seam line where necessary to make the appliqué lie flat. Concave curves may be clipped only; convex curves may be clipped in a "v" or actually notched (Fig. 2-34). It is unnecessary to turn under areas that will be covered by overlapping appliqué designs. Use a blindstitch and a thread that matches the appliqué.

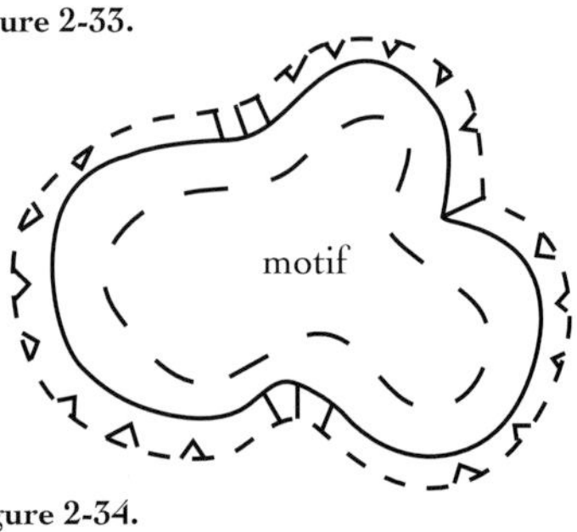

Figure 2-34.

BLINDSTITCH

With a threaded needle, come up from the motif back of the background fabric, through the edge turned under of the cutout chintz. Catch only a thread or two on the

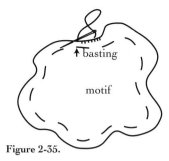

Figure 2-35.

very edge of the fold. Go directly back into the background fabric to the next tiny stitch, no more that ⅛" away (Fig. 2-35).

MY PREFERENCE

Traditional appliqué and I do not get along very well. So I prefer to use the blanket stitch. It allows the stitch to exaggerate, embellish, accentuate, decorate, and to change in length to take advantage of every little indentation. It adds embellishment to the motif, as well as covering its raw edge while firmly attaching it in place.

If you are more comfortable with the traditional appliqué, turn under the raw edges and go for it! I, of course, will never understand why, but so be it!

BLANKET STITCH

The blanket stitch is an embroidery term and a method of appliquéing fabric cutouts to the base or background fabric. If you are right-handed, work toward yourself. The needle enters the cutout on the outside edge of the design (seam line), and exits along the raw edge with the thread under the needle's point. This is a

Figure 2-36.
Blanket Stitch.

looped stitch. The thread forms a knot along the exit line, which is the raw edge (Fig. 2-36). The stitch rests on the cutout.

BUTTONHOLE STITCH

Often confused with the blanket stitch, the buttonhole stitch is different in the stitch and knot placement. The needle enters the cutout very near the raw edge and exits ⅛" to ¼" from the raw edge of the cutout through the base fabric. The thread loops over the needle tip. When completed, the knot rests along the raw edge with the stitch on the base fabric.

BLANKET STITCH REVISITED

You are finally ready for actual stitching. I would advise practicing on a small sample before diving into the quilt proper. (Just what you wanted to hear!)

1. Use a single thread and knot it at 18" to 20".

2. Work from right to the left if you are right-handed.

3. Start from the back of the background fabric and bring the needle up on the trimmed raw edge of the chintz cutout.

4. The needle's point goes down into the fabric at the printed edge of the motif.

5. The needle's point comes up at the trimmed edge of the cutout (Fig. 2-37) with the thread under the point of the needle).

Figure 2-37.
Buttonhole Stitch.

Figure 2-38.

6. Draw up the thread, keeping it as parallel to the fabric as possible, forming the knot (Fig. 2-38). This tends to make the resulting knot lay flat to the fabric.

7. Be consistent.

8. Keep stitches close.

9. Keep stitches at right angles to the motif edge.

TURNING CORNERS

Now some specifics to take advantage of all of the nuances in the printed motif. To smoothly stitch around scalloped edges, such as chrysanthemums or rose petals, create in your mind an invisible center point, and make all stitches directed toward it. All stitches seem to radiate from this invisible point and need not be the same length. Use them as embroidery details or embellishments (Fig. 2-39 and Fig. 2-40).

Figure 2-39.

←invisible center point

Figure 2-40.

The points of leaves or pointed petals render an opportunity to elongate the stitches, thus lengthening the points. These stitches, once again, radiate from an

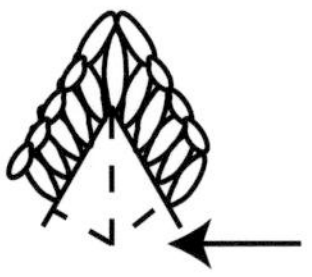

Figure 2-41.
Invisible center point.

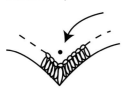

Figure 2-42.
Invisible center point, this time outside the motif.

invisible center (Fig. 2-41). Figure 2-42 shows the smooth execution of the blanket stitch covering an inside corner. Note, once again, the use of the invisible point, now on the outside of the appliquéd motif. After stitching around the corner point, petal completed, return as quickly as possible to right angle stitches (Fig. 2-43). This technique gives a consistency to the work. Remember, at all times, as with all needlework, keep your hands and work space clean. (No nibbling on the chocolate bonbons.)

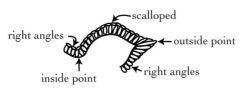

Figure 2-43.

APPLIQUÉ SEQUENCE

As in traditional appliqué, underneath pieces should be sewn down first. Then work up to the foreground. Trim motifs ⅛" from the printed edge as you approach the area to be worked. If you trim too far in advance, your hand will ravel the fabric as you sew. I trim only 1" or 2" ahead of my hand. To start the base element, roll back the foreground pieces. Start the blanket stitch just under the overlapping motif, two to three stitches under the overlay (Fig. 2-44).

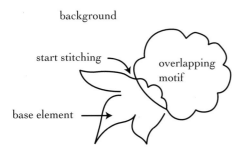

background

start stitching

overlapping motif

base element

Figure 2-44. *Overlapping motif rolled back to facilitate appliqué of base element.*

BACKGROUND

Figure 2-45.
Appliqué the overlay through the base element and background fabric.

Under most circumstances, when I blanket stitch the overlay, I usually go through the base motif and also through the background fabric. This makes it impossible to cut the background fabric away when the appliqué is completed (Fig. 2-45). Cutting away prematurely creates hazards.

Now, a warning regarding the trimming around the motif. *Do not trim* every little nuance; too much cutting away requires an excessive amount of blanket stitch, so much that the eye begins to see the stitch to the detriment of the floral element. I like to say, "trim away with grace." When trimming from one leaf to a neighbor, avoid a straight cut. A straight line is the shortest route between two points, but we want the most attractive cut. So trim gracefully, giving a slight indentation or curve to your cut (Fig. 2-46).

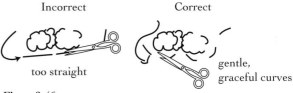

Incorrect

Correct

too straight

gentle, graceful curves

Figure 2-46.

When the motifs have been appliquéd in place, cut away the background material from the back of the work with small, sharp scissors. Appliqué shears with a pelican blade are ideal. Why cut away? Because you don't want to quilt through an extra layer! But cut carefully (Fig. 2-47)! As I was cutting (but not carefully enough) the background from beneath the center medallion of "Une Belle," I snipped and discarded and held up the quilt top. Lo and behold, I could look straight through. I had cut a neat and tidy hole in the motif. "Never fear," I said. "Thank you, Lord, that this is broderie perse!" I simply cut a posy from the remnants and buttonholed it into place. Today I really have to search for my patch..

Figure 2-47. *Wrong side of fabric and appliqué. Trim with extreme care.*

Plate 10. *"Une Belle Mademoiselle," 66½" x 67". Made by Barbara W. Barber, 1986.*

Plate 11. *"Tree of Life," 55½" x 63". Made by Barbara W. Barber, 1993. Made over a period of three years. This broderie perse "Tree of Life" is constructed to closely resemble the old Indian palampores. The photograph shows manipulation of border print to produce visual symmetry. The proliferation of quilted feathers surrounding the tree add interest to what would otherwise be empty background.*

Plate 12. *This quilt, 109" x 125", was donated to the Shelburne Museum in July 1969 by Henry Coger of Ashley Falls, MA. The center and parts between the borders are cut from early English floral glazed chintz and are appliquéd to a plain, off-white cotton. The inner and outer borders are of a glazed floral print chintz. At the bottom, on a strip between the center and the border, is a hand-quilted scroll with the name, "Sarah T. C. Miller 1830."*

Plate 13. *The former owner of this quilt reports that it was made in the Ridgley home, Baltimore, MD, for her grandmother before 1825. The makers were French. The quilt, 80" x 108", is constucted of twelve chintz appliquéd blocks. Each square has a different floral pattern in shades of blues, purples, and deep crimson on a white cotton background. The blocks are separated by bands of chintz.*

Plate 14. *A Tree of Life central motif spans the length of this eighteenth century quilt. The background of this quilt, 103" x 106", is of handwoven linen. The tree is made of brown linen printed motifs and the leaves are of blue printed cotton. The flowers and fruits are similar to pomegranates. The pheasants are cut from printed linen of many colors. On each side of the tree is a basket of flowers, roses, dahlias, two pineapples of green printed linen, a pheasant, and a vase with a bouquet of flowers. All the motifs are appliquéd. The border is of pointed scallops of indigo printed cotton with a tiny flower.*

Plate 15. *"Love," 36" x 40". Made by Louise Dutcher.*

Plate 16. *"Ode to Spring." Made by Gloria Greenlee.*

Plate 17. *"Centrifuge," 41" x 41". Made by Kitty Kurpiewski, Newington, Connecticut, 1991.*

Plate 18. *"Nosegay." Made by Judy Simmons. Collection of Museum of American Quilter's Society.*

Plate 19. *"Kensington Garden," 66" x 68". Made in ten months by Barbara W. Barber, 1988. Design influenced by Rose Kretsinger's "Paradise Garden."*

Plate 20. *"Mist & Shadows," 80" x 85". Made by Laura Crews.*

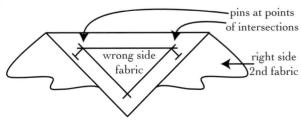
...ING ...worked
sepa... ...d outer
borders. O... ...pt for the
corners of the in... ...the parts.
This is really gratifying ... usually proceeds at a snail's pace.

PRECISION PIECING

Each quilt part should have stitching lines marked on
the wrong side. These were drawn when the exact measurements were determined and transferred to fabric
(Review Chapter 2).

Point to point:

• With right sides of the fabric together pin point-to-
point by "point," the intersecting corners on the
marked stitching line (Fig. 3-1). Pin at the points of
intersection.

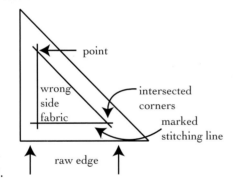

Figure 3-1.

• Align seam lines back and front, by inserting pins
and checking to ascertain that the pins exit seam
lines on the back side of the second piece. Add pins
along the stitching line with the pins running along
(not across) the seam lines of both the back and
front pieces (Fig. 3-2).

Figure 3-2.

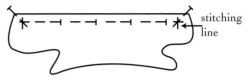

Figure 3-3.

• Stitch on the seam line only. Also, never sew over a
previously sewn seam. Carefully following this
process will result in miters and seams that lay flat.

ASSEMBLING THE CENTER MEDALLION

Sew an appropriate seam to the point of intersection and end the seam. Move the seam allowances
aside. Once past the seam, begin stitching again and
proceed to the end point.

Assemble in the following sequence:

1. Add the inner
border (2, 3, 4, 5) to
the center diamond,
matching all points
and stitching lines
(Fig. 3-4).

2. Sew miters
of first inner bor-
der, being sure to
sew only point-to-
point, not into the
seam allowance.

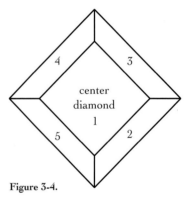

Figure 3-4.

3. Add the four triangles to achieve a square configuration.

4. Add the second inner border pieces and complete the miters.

5. Then do the insets and the miters of the insets.

6. Next complete the outer borders and miters.

7. After stitching, trim the seam allowances to ¼".
Press well, pressing open the miter seams. Press the
border seams toward the borders.

8. Complete the broderie perse by appliquéing in
place the motifs over the mitered seams of the insets
(Plate 21, page 34).

9. Now trim away from behind the final corner
motifs. Even the mitered seam may be trimmed to within ¼" of the stitching.

Plate 21. *"Une Belle Mademoiselle." Motifs appliquéd over miter.*

add a 3-D effect. In addition I used metallic gold and added outline stitches to some of the veins. I also used French knots for the rose centers and to simulate dew on the leaves.

I could have added the small and intricate feathery flower sprays that I had deleted from the chintz cutouts (Fig. 3-6). Little feathery branches with tiny forget-me-not flowers can be added with either fine, one-strand embroidery floss or by utilizing an extra fine-tip, permanent pen. By merely touching the very tip of the pen to the fabric, and by using a very light

Figure 3-6.

touch, the look of pen and ink of the nineteenth century is achieved. I have done this on a miniature "Kensington Garden". The size of the quilt and the intricate design mandated embellishment in addition to the broderie perse application.

My appliqué and motif could not have been small enough in scale to carry out the design, so pen and ink drawing became a viable option. I have drawn wonderful, feathery wheat heads, small vines, curlicues, daisies, and buds on other appliqué quilts. This technique adds great depth and interest (Fig. 3-7).

It takes nerves of steel to add this kind of embellishment to a complet-

Figure 3-7.

ed piece! The good news is, if a mistake occurs, it can be turned into a daisy or a curly vine.

When I worked on "Tree of Life," I embellished with DMC machine embroidery thread. I used stitches that lent themselves to the printed fabric — chain, outline, blanket — to accent the flowers and stems. This time I was pleased with the results which gave a fascinating 3-D appearance to the tree. It brought to mind the cutwork that Grandma tried to teach me years ago. "Kensington" received none of this preferential treatment, poor thing!

10. Now, pat yourself on the back; you have done a good piece of work!

SPECIAL TOUCHES

After the quilt top is completed, hang it up, step back, and look at your handiwork objectively. I know that is hard to do, something like asking a mother to step back and impartially look at her own child. At this time decide if embellishing the quilt will add to it or detract from it. As I was pressing the top of "Une Belle" for the last time, I thought of embellishing it. Did I really want to do this? No, I really did not. But once I have an idea, very often I find myself unable to talk myself out of it.

A close look will reveal that I did embellish the veins in the leaves and various parts of the roses (Fig. 3-5) with embroidery. I selected embroidery

outline stitch

chain stitch

french knots

Figure 3-5.

floss that closely matched the colors of the areas to be embellished. In fact I matched it so closely that it is hard to see my work except for the fact that it does

SIGNING

Be sure to sign your name and date to the front of your quilt. A nice touch is embroidering with thread that matches the quilt background color. Tone on tone is always understated and ritzy. Are you presumptuous enough to add the date prematurely? Signing and dating your masterpiece increases its value, both now and in the future (Plate 22).

Plate 22. *Signing and dating your quilt.*

QUILTING DESIGN TECHNIQUES

Congratulations! You have completed your quilt top! I am proud of you!

This has probably taken anywhere from a few months to several years. Just when you feel you have finished, it's time to begin the next phase of your masterpiece, the quilting. We will look ahead to quilting designs, inspirations, and possibilities. Good sources of inspiration are quilt magazines and books for design ideas selected by others. Also, take a good look at fabrics you have used in the construction of the quilt. Can any design elements be used or adapted?

ADAPTING FABRIC DESIGN

Take a hint from your fabric design. The print can sometimes be simplified and/or adapted into a quilting design. I picked out the chintz fabric for "Kensington Garden" because I especially liked the bunch of grapes in it. Immediately I knew I would adapt those grapes for the quilting design. I did exactly that. Only after I quilted ten or more bunches of these grapes in the swags did I realize they were gooseberries, not grapes! The grapes stayed anyway.

PURCHASED TEMPLATES

Purchased template designs traced onto paper can be enlarged or reduced on a copy machine. When the correct size and/or scale is achieved, cut a new plastic template with a craft knife. Use the purchased template as a guide.

FEATHER DESIGNS

Consider a feather design. You can never go wrong with feathers. They add grace to a quilt.

DESIGNING FOR SPECIFIC AREAS

Cut a piece of paper the exact size and shape of your quilting design area (Fig. 3-8).

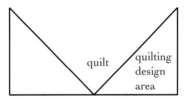

Figure 3-8.

Many commercial feather templates are available for purchase, and there are also some very good books and quilt magazine articles devoted to drafting feather designs. Just keep in mind that they must always have a graceful curve to their vine.

For "Une Belle Mademoiselle,", I folded my corner design paper pattern in half (Fig. 3-9). Drawing an asymmetrical feather on half of the large triangle will produce a symmetrical design when it is duplicated on the second half.

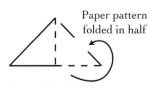

Figure 3-9.

To begin the feather, draw a graceful stem, allowing ample room for the fronds (Fig. 3-10).

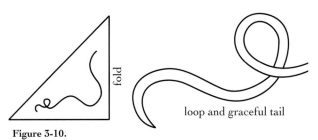

Figure 3-10.

loop and graceful tail

To finish off a formal feather design, include at least one loop and a graceful curl at the tail end of the stem. These touches add elegance to the entire piece.

Place a series of fronds along the curve of the stem. Coins of various sizes make good patterns (Fig. 3-11).

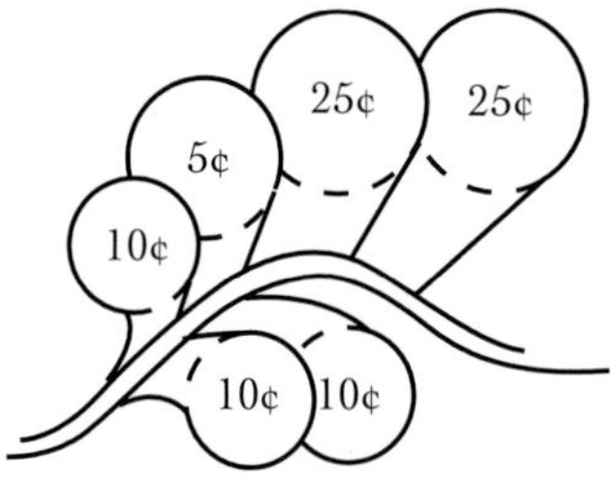

Figure 3-11.

A primitive feather would have no loop at the tail end, just a slight curl to the tail. All the fronds would be of equal size (Fig. 3-12).

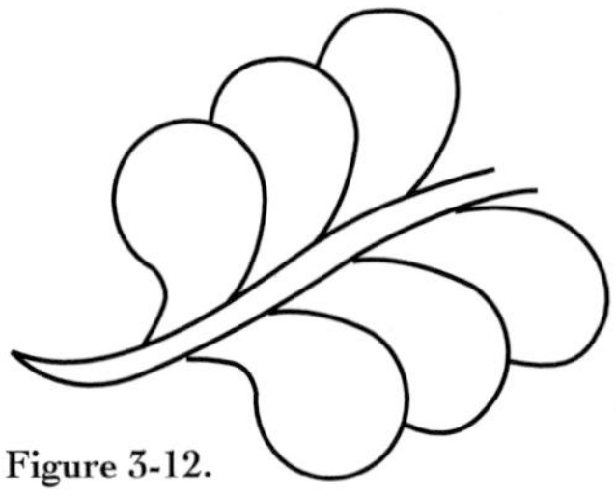

When your feather is just right, you will know. It will have the feel to your artistic eye like the just right feel of pie crust in the hands of a successful pie maker.

Figure 3-12.

A SWAG FULL OF FEATHERS

This is the pattern I used on the "Kensington Garden" swags.

First, I duplicated the swag exactly on paper, including the appliqué line of adjoining colors. I folded this paper swag pattern in half to establish the center of the swag (Fig. 3-13).

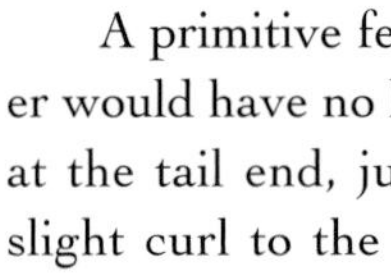

Figure 3-13.

On this particular swag, the stem is optical only. The fronds actually grow from the stem or appliqué lines of adjoining colors. Once again using coins, in this case dimes, I

filled the area with fronds that decrease in size appropriate to the diminishing swag dimension. These fronds were planned on half of the total swag (Fig. 3-14).

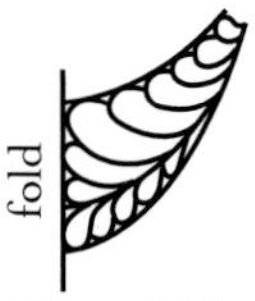

Once I was satisfied with my feathers and fronds, I then traced them onto the other side of the pattern by the use of a light box (Fig. 3-15). Satisfied with the attractive results, I proceeded to cut out a plastic template.

Figure 3-14.

Figure 3-15.

TRANSFER DESIGN

To transfer the quilting design to your quilt top, first tape the paper design securely to a light box. Place your quilt top over the box, carefully and precisely placing the area to be marked. Secure with pins or tape, depending on your light box.

You can make a light box if you do not have one. For years, I set the glass portion (freshly cleaned) of my front storm door, supported by six cans of cat food, on my dining room table. I nestled a mechanic's trouble light between the table and glass. It worked quite well.

TRACING

Once the quilting design and quilt are mounted in place, trace the design in pencil with a light hand. Turn the light off after the first few marks to judge the appropriate strength of the pencil lines. The tendency is to mark too darkly when using a light box, so take care.

MAKING A PLASTIC TEMPLATE

Occasionally a quilting design cannot be traced. This happens when the background fabric is very dark, and the design cannot be seen, even with a light box. Plastic templates come in handy.

SUPPLIES:

Template plastic
Extra fine permanent pen
Craft knife
Quilting design (Fig. 3-16, page 38)

Use a cushion of several newspapers to protect your work surface. Place your paper quilt design on the newspapers and your template plastic over the design. With your craft knife, carefully cut a channel

Quilting design
for "Une Belle Mademoiselle."

bottom of triangle

feather template
"Une Belle Mademoiselle"

fold

wide enough to accommodate a marking pencil. Remember to leave bridges when you cut or your whole design will fall out of the template plastic (Fig. 3-17).

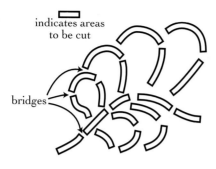

indicates areas to be cut

bridges

Figure 3-17.

MARKING AND PREPARING TO QUILT

Because we are constructing a quilt of heirloom quality, the choice of marking medium is of utmost importance. The antique chintz quilts have existed 100 years or more without being washed. Washing tends to remove the glaze. As with the very special heirloom quilts of generations past, I personally have no intention of washing mine. So, my method of marking the top is of utmost importance. I have to use something that will last long enough to quilt the design and no longer. I want no markings left or any residue.

MARKING MEDIUM

Mechanical pencils specifically made for marking quilts are the best choice. They have a marking medium that contains no oil unlike ordinary lead. Ultimate Marking Pencil for Quilters® is one such commercial marker. Take care not to mark the design with a heavy hand. This is appropriate for light backgrounds. For darker fabrics use a Berol® white or yellow pencil. After using a silver Berol on black, I was dismayed to find that the camera's lens picked it up, even after it had disappeared to the naked eye.

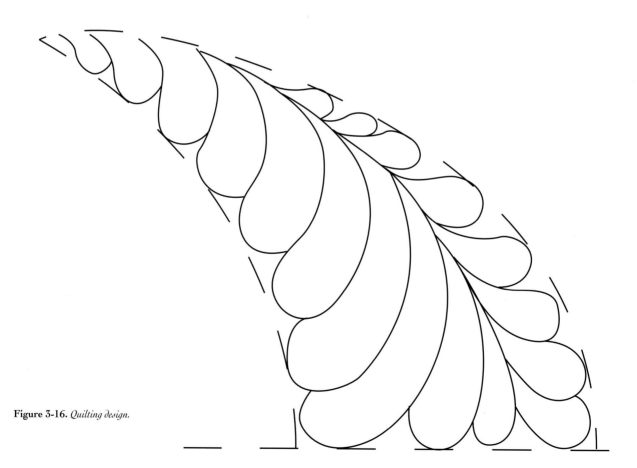

Figure 3-16. *Quilting design.*

When I made "Kensington Garden" in 1988, I was unaware of the dangers of masking tape (even quilter's tape is of the same nature). Using tape as a guideline seemed very easy. But there are drawbacks. Tape leaves a residue on the fabric not visible to the naked eye but sufficient to pick up eventual discoloration.

The process of removing the tape from the fabric tends to draw the polyester fibers along with the adhesive, working themselves through the fabric. Once this migration begins, it tends to increase with time, and with use. It creates a furry appearance on its surface, visibly aging the quilt. Not realizing these disadvantages, I did use tape on "Kensington." Quilting along the tape my stitches tended to be larger than usual. Evidently, the tape introduces a stiffness that prohibits manipulation.

After the grid hand quilting was completed, I knew I needed to do better. I removed the stitches, one row at a time, and did them over. As the stitches were removed from the unwashed chintz, each row was clearly marked with needle holes, so I just quilted again, using the holes as my guide. I know, more time than sense! So, as far as marking goes, what's left: back to the marking pencil.

BACKGROUND QUILTING DESIGNS

Regardless of what the background quilting design will be, it is necessary to anchor around the perimeter of each motif. A row of outline quilting, approximately ⅛" from the edge of the motif accomplishes this. If appliqués are clustered and several appliqués are superimposed upon each other, quilt around each motif within the cluster. Quilting selected sections within the motifs will anchor the motifs even more (Fig. 3-18). No large areas are left unquilted.

Figure 3-18.

That said, the overall background quilting is next. Traditional background quilting choices, or fillings, are used to cover background areas and/or accentuate other quilting designs. All are executed with small running stitches. See the examples in Figure 3-19.

MARKING CHEVRONS

The design I used for background quilting "Kensington Garden" could be called a chevron grid. It has equidistant horizontal and vertical lines meeting at an

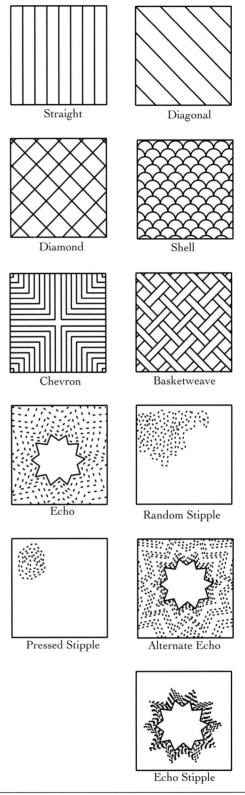

Straight   Diagonal

Diamond   Shell

Chevron   Basketweave

Echo   Random Stipple

Pressed Stipple   Alternate Echo

Echo Stipple

Figure 3-19. *Background quilting designs.*

angle (Fig. 3-21). Such a pattern seems simple and really can be, providing the quilt is truly square, and the work progresses on a well organized plan.

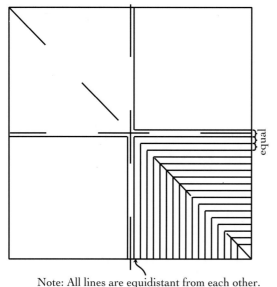

Note: All lines are equidistant from each other. This means that from the center lines to the first chevron line, it is a half-size increment.

Figure 3-20.

On a grid plan and in the designer's vision, everything is square, dimensionally accurate, and the right angles are a true 90°. The quilt being assembled often is an imperfect reflection of that ideal. But do not worry. Artists have many options available to make it come out right!

First find the center of each side and mark it. This divides the quilt into four quadrants or squares. Also, mark the diagonals; corner to corner, passing precisely through the quilt's center (Fig. 3-22).

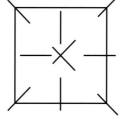

Figure 3-21.

This diagonal line will keep the chevron lined up. A 90° angle must occur on this line every time.

The ideal square quilt may deviate due to the very nature of fabric. For this reason, after the initial quadrants and diagonals have been marked, I temporarily mark the increments with pins, one quadrant at a time.

Establish the increments (I used 1"), measure from the center of one side out toward the edge of the quilt side, and toward the top or bottom.

Because all the lines are equidistant from each other, it is important to note that from the center lines to the first chevron line (either side of center), must be a half-size increment (Fig. 3-23).

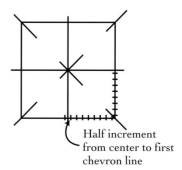

Figure 3-22.

↳ Half increment
from center to first
chevron line

To facilitate the measurement and establishing the increments, use a clean carpenter's square. Place the 90° angle on the diagonal, marking temporarily with pins on the diagonal and the edges.

Resist the temptation to measure and mark increments on the diagonal. They will not and should not be the same increment as on the outside edge. The increment will be greater along the diagonal line.

I do temporary marks until I am assured that I end in the corner of each quadrant. with the identical size square (Fig. 3-24). A slight deviation of lines will go unnoticed, but ending with anything other than a perfect square in the corner will be readily noticeable.

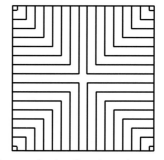

Figure 3-23. *The corner of each quadrant is a perfect square.*

It's easier to move a pin, and "fudge" the line slightly, than to have marked with pencil and find out it is incorrect.

When satisfied that the pins (temporary markings) are correctly placed, then mark with the pencil, removing the pins incrementally as you do.

PREPARING THE BACKING

Hopefully you have two lengths of backing fabric on hand if you need to piece the backing.

The temptation will be to simply seam two lengths down the center and proceed. Let's rethink that impulse. The quilt will hang more evenly if you have a width down the center and then seam a split length onto each side (Fig. 3-25). Some thought should go into where these seams fall. They should

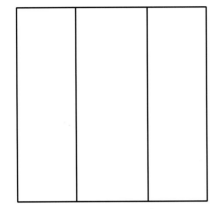

Figure 3-24. *Backing fabric with seams.*

correspond with the front background design to give it a professional appearance. Trim off any selvages. You don't really want to quilt through them, do you? Press the seams open and flat. The back should measure approximately 2" larger than the front on all the sides.

BATTING

Next comes the batting. Spread it evenly and smoothly to get rid of any wrinkles. (Opening the package a day or two previous to use helps "fluff" it out.) Sometimes it needs to be smoothed out when on the backing. Use a yardstick to smooth when pulling and readjusting gets tough. It does help!

After spreading the batting out on the backing, trim it the size of the backing.

I prefer a very thin batt — one conducive to intensive, close hand quilting. My preferences are:

Hobbs Thermore™ ("Tree of Life") and

Mountain Mist Lite™ ("Une Belle Mademoiselle" and "Kensington Garden").

SOURCE:

Hancock's
3841 Hinkleville Road
Paducah, KY 42001
800-626-2723 (24 hours)

Basting Bee

*"Quilters get along so well
because they leave their egos at the door;
they create a community of helping."*
—Rose Korteski

CHAPTER FOUR

ut on the teapot, make a bunch of cookies, and invite your quilting friends in to lend a hand. After spending a considerable amount of time producing a quilt top, what better way to show off your work to an appreciative audience of quilt friends than inviting them in for a basting bee. Not only is it more fun to have a communal bee, but it is certainly more productive to set up the frame, stretch out the three layers, and to have help turning and keeping the tension constant. One set of quilter's hands is not quite enough. The opportunity to socialize when inviting friends in to help with the basting is of enough importance to perpetuate the bee tradition.

As in the earlier days of our country, the quilting or basting bee is an opportunity to exchange recipes, quilting patterns and hints, happenings, concerns about husbands and kids. (Would that be considered gossip? Of course not!) It is a time to enjoy each other's company while doing what quilters do best — making needles fly.

As I read about the bees of years past, I am more and more convinced that they were the forerunner of our modern day group therapy sessions. In fact, the current tying or basting goes a long way toward providing that same strength. The bond produced by such groups supersedes merely quilting interests. In quilting bees of long ago the more experienced were always allowed to work on the extra special quilts. The less experienced, or drones as they were called, were given kitchen duty! Children got to thread the needles. Would we be as selective today? I've found that any quilter, at whatever stage of expertise, is a more than willing helper. I for one appreciate any and all volunteers.

BASTING THE QUILT

When we reach the basting stage, the three layers of the quilt sandwich are ready. The backing has been pieced and pressed well with the piecing seams pressed open. The batt package has been open and spread out for a day or so to remove wrinkles. The top (definitely a masterpiece) is well pressed and marked with the quilting design.

THE FRAME

A basting or tying frame is the best way to assemble the three layers. A quilt basting frame is made up of two sets of rails — the longer frame rails and the shorter "rolling" rails (fig 4-1). The quilt sandwich is attached to these four rails, and as the basting proceeds, it is rolled around the shorter rails. I am fortunate to have several old sets of quilt frames, now much coveted by antique dealers. Using them as a guide, a set could easily be made.

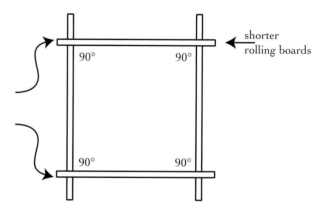

Figure 4-1. *A quilt basting frame.*

Purchase four pieces of 1' x 3' lumber — long, strong, straight, and smooth — and four C clamps. Two of the boards should be 8' long and the other two, 6'. Of course, if you are looking to the future and using this for the basting or tying of larger quilts, all four boards could be 8'. Sand the edges until smooth. Along the edge of the boards, securely staple strips of double muslin or ticking. These strips are cut 2" wide and as long as the boards. Staple the strips to the boards at regular, close intervals with a staple gun. It is to this fabric that the quilt backing will be pinned. Take time now to mark the midpoint of each board. (I drove a tack into each board for a permanent reference.)

The frames are supported at the corners with tripods, chair backs, or legs, high enough for the quilters' comfort. For true 90° corners, check them with a clean carpenter's square. If the frame is not square, neither will your quilt be (Fig. 4-2).

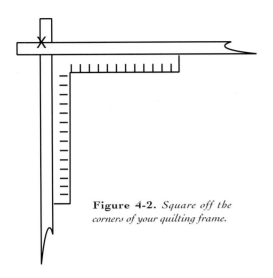

Figure 4-2. *Square off the corners of your quilting frame.*

MOUNTING

Opposite sides of the backing (and later the top) should be placed, stretched, and pinned simultaneously in order to maintain proper alignment of all of the elements. Match the centers of the quilt backing (all four sides) to the centers of the quilt frame boards — the length first and then the width.

Spread the backing to the frame wrong side up, not too tightly but taut enough to be almost flat. Allow the raw edges to proceed to the outside edge of the frame boards the extra 2" previously mentioned. Pin with the pins parallel to the shorter rolling boards, to facilitate the rolling process (Fig. 4-3).

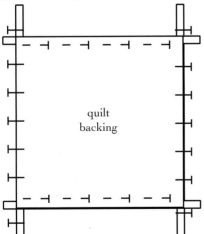

quilt backing

Figure 4-3. *Pinning the quilt to the frame.*

Spread and smooth the batting over the backing, and then center the quilt top over the backing and batting. It should reach to the pinning tape on the frame boards.

BASTING

When all is straight, square, and tidy, it's time to start the basting. Do not use odd lots of colored, unused thread for basting! Once, and only once, I used some old blue thread. When I removed it, after the quilting was completed, it left little blue dots that could not be removed. So be advised! Quite often I use white quilting thread for basting. I use long lengths and back-stitch or knot at the end. If you have remembered to position the pins parallel to the rolling boards, it will keep the quilt fabrics from catching on the pins as the quilt is rolled.

Millinery needles are handy tools for basting. They are easy to thread, and their long length makes it easier to pierce all three layers and return to the surface neatly and quickly. Baste parallel to all boards at 3" to 4" increments, producing an overall grid of basting (Fig. 4-4).

After basting several rows, or as far as you can comfortably reach, it is time to "roll" the quilt. The sides of the quilt must be loosened near the rolling board, releasing the fabric.

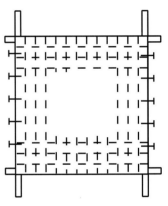

Figure 4-4. *Basting.*

Release the clamps holding the rolling board in place. Roll only one board at a time. Roll the basted part under, and clamp the rolling board in place again.

Station a person at each corner of the frame to hold the side boards in place. This will prevent a disaster from the frame collapsing. Those at the corners need to hold firmly while the cross boards are rolled one at a time. It is important to maintain the tension of the three layers and keep the quilt squared.

Rolling allows those basting to reach farther and farther toward the center. The basting and rolling process is continued until the quilt is completely basted.

By standing at the frame, those basting can reach farther so the quilt does not have to be rolled as much. This is helpful since rolling does wrinkle fabric and can distort it.

Remove all pins, rest your back, and get ready for the next step.

Hand Quilting

I always anticipate arriving at the hand quilting stage in the construction of a quilt. At this point most quilt related decisions have been made. I simply let my fingers do the quilting, and I let my mind run rampant to my next quilt…and the next…and…

NEEDLES AND THREAD

It is true, the smaller the quilting needle, the smaller the quilting stitch. I quilt with #12 quilting needles. The Japanese #12 are shorter and slimmer than others, but often more difficult to find. I am partial to Coats Dual Duty cotton-covered polyester quilting thread.

LAP QUILTING

Personally, I find it convenient to remove the quilt from the basting frame and work on it in my lap without a hoop or frame. But there are other options.

Many commercial quilting frames are available. A quilter need only read any of the popular quilt magazines on the market today to encounter a number of advertisements for a variety of frames in a wide price range. A quilting frame always looks so homey. It does keep the work readily available. A drawback is the amount of space it occupies. Instructions for attaching the three layers of the quilt sandwich to the frames are included with a frame purchase.

Hoops are another option for maintaining tension on the quilt sandwich while stitching. They take up very little room and are portable. They can be held on the lap, supported on a table, or attached to a stand. The big advantage of a hoop is that it can be turned so the quilter can work in any direction.

No matter whether you prefer a hoop or a frame, begin at the quilt center and work outward. As previously discussed in chapter 3, it is necessary to anchor around the perimeter of each motif. A row of outline quilting approximately ⅛" from the edge of the motif will accomplish this.

If the appliqué is clustered and several appliqués are superimposed upon each other, quilt around each motif within the cluster. Quilting selected areas within the motif will anchor it even more. All the large areas should be anchored. Wherever your quilt center is,

apply these recommendations and work toward the perimeter. In addition to anchoring the motifs, individual quilting motifs such as feathers, are quilted before the surrounding background is done.

THE STITCH

When executing the hand-quilting stitch, the stitches and the spaces between should be evenly done. The little dimples that the stitches create should be uniformly spaced. Also, it should be impossible to tell where each length of thread begins and ends. Both knots and backstitching should be invisible.

Begin by making a knot in the end of an 8" to 10" thread. Wrap the tail of your thread around the tip of the threaded needle two or three times. Then draw the needle through the wraps while holding the wrapped thread with your thumb and forefinger (Fig. 5-1).

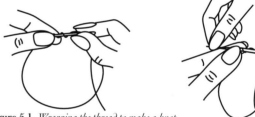

Figure 5.1. *Wrapping the thread to make a knot.*

Insert the needle into the background fabric of the quilt top through the batting. Exit ½" from the point of entry and at the beginning of the quilting line. Jerk gently until the knot pops (you can hear it) through the top fabric and lodges in the batting.

While manipulating the fabric, push the needle with your thimble-covered middle finger, taking several small running stitches. To produce tiny stitches, go back into the fabric as soon as the needle is barely visible.

Stitch until approximately three inches of thread remain. I know it's always a temptation to take just a few more stitches until, alas, the needle unthreads!

Thread again with your threader to finish off.
- Make your last stitch a "mini" (Fig. 5-2).
- Reverse the needle direction through the sandwich area. Exit the needle at the beginning of a stitch three or four stitches back (Fig. 5-3).
- Make a single knot in the thread near the quilt sur-

face. Slip the needle through the thread loop and pull gently, making a knot (Fig. 5-4).

•Insert the needle where you last exited, going back on the other side of the stitches, and exit at the mini stitch. Clip the thread (Fig. 5-5).

•To begin the next thread insert the needle ½" from the mini stitch beginning. Exit the needle at the beginning of the mini stitch and proceed (Fig. 5-6).

Using this method, you will have consecutive quilting stitches on the top and back of your quilt.

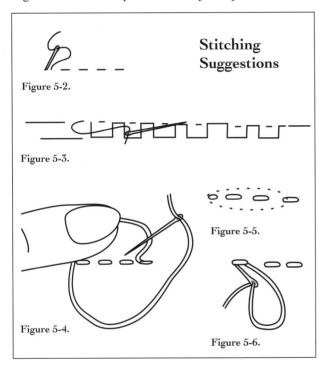

Stitching Suggestions

Figure 5-2.

Figure 5-3.

Figure 5-4.

Figure 5-5.

Figure 5-6.

It is a given that every stitch needs to go through all three layers. I need to have my left thumb under the quilt at all times to feel the prick of the needle to make sure I have done this. Naturally, this leads to permanently mutilated fingertips on that "under-the-quilt" hand. I've tried all the new contraptions that have been invented to protect those delicate fingertips, but I'm uncomfortable with all of them. Someone recommended moleskin in such glowing terms that I tried that, only to quilt right through it. I virtually sewed my fingers to the back of the quilt. I've also heard that eventually a callous develops, but after 20 years of intense quilting, even that hasn't occurred. My fingers are just under there, pricked and mutilated. Naturally, I occasionally bleed on the quilt. (It's not a quilt until it's bled on, the old axiom goes.) The best way to remove blood is to have a "spitball" of threads ready. Rub the spot with the spitball, and your saliva will remove your blood.

ECHO STIPPLE QUILTING

Stipple quilting, as I prefer to do it, might be referred to as using close echo quilting. It is time consuming, mesmerizing, and very effective. It gives texture to the area and embosses the motifs it surrounds. The advantage is not having to mark the design.

The first row of quilting follows the configuration of the motif. This includes feathers and other quilted designs. Each subsequent row is approximately ⅛" from the previous row (Fig. 5-7).

Each indentation of the motif must be emphasized.

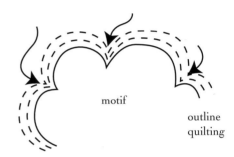

motif

outline quilting

Figure 5-7.

EXAGGERATED INDENTATIONS

As each row of quilting is added following the previously established row, exaggerations must be repeated at the points of indentation (Fig. 5-8).

At every indentation, or "v" in a quilting row, make the stitch at that point closer than the established ⅛".

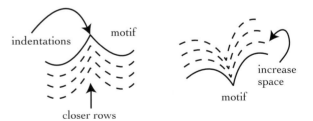

indentations   motif

closer rows

increase space

motif

Figure 5-8.   Figure 5-9.

THE FLIP SIDE

On outside curves, increase the space between rows a slight amount (Fig. 5-9).

These techniques and their variations add interest. Otherwise, the quilting lines tend to straighten out and lose shape and interest.

As the indentations are filled, the pattern begins to develop, like clouds in the sky.

MULTIPLE NEEDLES

For large areas, thread a double length of thread through two needles. Begin in the center of a wide area and work outward. This allows the use of longer pieces of thread, creating half as many starts and stops (Fig. 5-10).

Figure 5-10. *Use threaded needles at both ends.*

Instead of quilting one row at a time, thread several needles (Fig. 5-11). Rather than quilting one line as far as the thread will go, quilt several inches in the immediate area. Leave the needle and thread in place, go back and pick up the next needle and go forward. Many times I have up to six needles at work simultaneously.

An encouraging effect of this method is that the quilted area appears more quickly than it would by quilting one row at a time. I utilized this mind game while quilting the large background areas of "Tree of Life.". The stipple quilting appeared to be completed faster by working with several needles simultaneously around the tree, than by one row at a time.

Figure 5-11. *Quilting rows made with several needles.*

EQUIDISTANT ROWS

As the rows of quilting around the motifs build up, it is important to have them meet in the center of any and every given area (Fig 5-12).

The viewer's eye will definitely pick up if the rows do not meet in the center.

In some obvious areas, I actually measure and run a line of basting to ascertain that my rows do meet where I want (Fig. 5-13). It may be necessary to add an extra row on one side or the other of the center. That will not be obvious, but off center definitely will.

halfway points

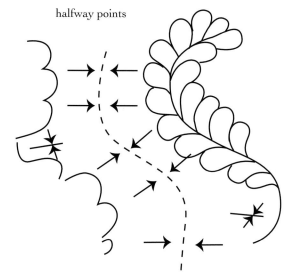

Figure 5-12. *The rows of quilting should match.*

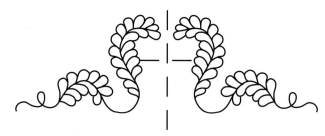

Figure 5-13. *Measure and baste to find center.*

One very specific area where preplanning and marking paid off was in the feathers of "Une Belle,"as noted.

They say there is an exception to every rule. This is true here, too.

When quilting around a given motif and working out to a border, continue working outward.

To add interest in "Tree of Life," I exaggerated the space between my rows in my rush to the border. I like the effect (Fig. 5-14).

One hazard or drawback of intense quilting is the tendency to "draw up" the quilt. Do not draw your thread tightly.

Also remember that intense quilting in one area usually calls for lots of quilting in all areas. So commit to that.

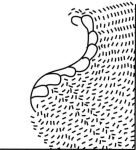

Figure 5-14. *Intense quilting.*

"Sleep with a quilt, it's safer."
— Barbara Barber

CHAPTER SIX

Trapunto

*N*ow that the quilting is complete, we will move on to trapunto. Trapunto is an Italian word meaning "stuffed work." Certain areas of the design are stuffed so that they stand out in bas-relief against the quilted background. This technique has long been used to draw attention and to give opulence and elegance to the overall quilt design. Why do the trapunto after the quilting? Because then the quilt will tell you just how much to stuff. Areas within the stipple quilting, especially, will appear to be deflated balloons. Stuff them just enough to inflate them and no more. Otherwise, the fabric will become distorted.

METHODS

When constructing "Une Belle," I had no idea how to do trapunto. I consulted a quilt glossary: "Make balls of cotton and insert them into the desired areas," the glossary indicated. The following methods were suggested:

1. Baste and quilt marked top to a thin gauze-like fabric. Stuff through that thin fabric. Then proceed to assemble with batting and backing. Quilt again around the stuffed areas.

2. Assemble the three layers of the quilt. Quilt as desired, then slit the backing, stuff through the slit, and whipstitch it. Many antique quilts were made using this method.

The first method sounded like a lot of duplication of effort to me. And I didn't want slits on the back of my quilt. Instead I came up with my own method.

Assemble the quilt and complete quilting. Then separate the threads of the backing fabric, stuff, and put the displaced threads back in their original place. Yes, this is the technique for me. There are no holes, and the method is simple.

SUPPLIES

Good grade polyester stuffing

Toothpicks, round to make small openings in the quilt back and thin, rectangular ones for poking

Crewel needle, #16

Acrylic, worsted weight yarn

Clean pliers

FRONDS

I started by sharpening the smallest diameter and most pointed round toothpicks I could find. By utilizing a twisting and screwing action, I was able to make a very small opening in the quilt backing. Then I was able to catch a small amount of cotton on the toothpick and start feeding it through the backing and batting materials. Note that the filling must lay on top of the batting to prevent quilt distortion.

This process proved to be very tedious, and quite disappointing. I used this method briefly while stuffing the feathers within "Une Belle." Each frond took 15 minutes. After doing only one or two, I counted the total number of fronds and then multiplied them out only to realize that I wouldn't live long enough to complete them. I took a crochet hook #0 and removed the cotton through the original holes.

In my next process I used polyfil stuffing. This material was much better to work with, since I was able to spread it out into thin strings, almost as fine as the thread used in spinning. Again I used a toothpick for stuffing. This time, I selected a thin rectangular toothpick. The round ones were too wide. The toothpick was rough enough to hold the polyfil and draw it right into the frond. Getting the polyfil straight through the batting was easy. Once the toothpick pierced the batting, it left an opening for the stuffing to follow. I had to hold it there with my thumb and finger while I took out the toothpick to use again (Fig. 6-1). Stuffing with the toothpick and polyfil cut my time per frond down to

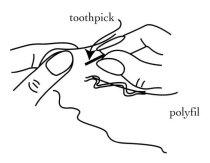

Figure 6-1.   Holding the already inserted polyfil with thumb and finger

three minutes. Completion of this project now seemed possible within the foreseeable future!

After the frond is stuffed, use the toothpick or the point of a pin to move the threads of the quilt backing back into place. Then close the hole. Change the toothpick often; the roughness of a new one makes stuffing easier. Be careful not to overstuff.

STEMS

Thread a crewel needle #16 with acrylic worsted weight yarn. Starting as close as possible to the quilted point of the stem channel, insert the threaded needle. Move it around through the channel on top of the batting.

Manipulate the needle as far as possible, making sure to come out and go in around loops. Come out through the backing, leaving a ½" tail at the point of

entry. Get a good grip on the needle with the clean pliers, and draw the yarn through the channels. Do not draw too tightly to avoid puckering. Go back in through your exit hole and proceed. Now come out from the stem (Fig. 6-2).

Leave ½" tails until all the fronds and feathers are completely stuffed. Check the work to make sure that there is absolutely no puckering. Any flaws can be worked out of the stem by rolling the raised materials between very clean fingertips. Additional yarn from these tails may be worked in to improve the feature. This done, snip yarn close to the backing, work the yarn ends into the quilt and out of sight. Close the hole by moving threads back into place with the toothpick or a pin.

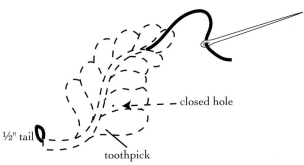

Figure 6-2.

Plate 23. *"Tree of Life," detail.*

"Excellence is shown by how hard we work
when no one else is looking."
— Barbara Barber

CHAPTER SEVEN

Now that you have finished with the appliqué, quilting, and trapunto, we can move on to the finishing. This chapter will discuss the making and application of binding. Several options are presented. Also consider making a sleeve. And last, but certainly not least, is the content of the label and its applications. The end is in sight!

MAKING THE BINDING

Quilt "law" says a bias binding is best and, of course, it is for curved edges. However, I continue to prefer bindings cut on the straight grain of the fabric. The finished width of the bindings on my chintz quilts is ⅜". I make a double binding, which is cut six times the desired finished width. The formula is: ⅜" x 6" = 2¼". I prefer to cut straight binding parallel to the selvage for less give when it is applied to the quilt. To make continuous binding, join the right sides of the short ends of two binding strips from corner to corner (Fig. 7-1). Trim the seam allowance to ¼". Press open. Continue to add more binding strips until the strip is as long as the perimeter of the quilt, plus 12" for the corners and for joining the binding edges. Press the binding in half lengthwise, wrong sides together, to produce the double-fold binding.

APPLYING THE BINDING

Leaving a 4" tail of binding, sew the doubled binding to the quilt top with the raw edges of the binding and raw edges of the quilt aligned. Use a ⅜" seam allowance. Stop sewing ⅜" from the corner, and then backstitch (Fig. 7-2). Use a walking foot, if you have one. Remove the needle from the quilt. Cut the threads and take the quilt out from the machine. Fold the binding up, forming a 45° angle from the quilt corner (Fig. 7-3). Then fold the binding back down even with the edge of the quilt (Fig. 7-4).

Beginning at the edge of the binding fabric and using a ⅜" seam allowance, sew several stitches and then backstitch. Continue sewing to the next corner. Repeat this procedure at each corner and sew the bind-

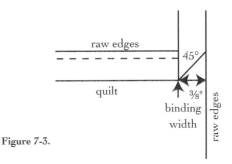

Figure 7-3.

Figure 7-4.

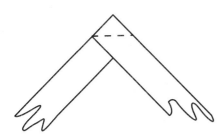

Figure 7-1. *Joining straight binding strips.*

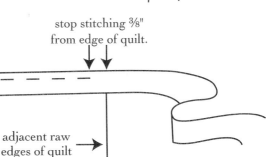

Figure 7-2. *Applying the binding to the quilt.*

ing to within 8" of the start. Next measure the binding "tails" still to be applied to the quilt. Join the ends of the binding corner to corner in the same way the binding strips were attached (Fig. 7-5).

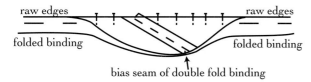

Figure 7-5.

I pin these two strips temporarily for proper placement before actually stitching them. Trim the binding joint to ¼" seam allowance. Press open. Complete sewing the binding to the quilt (Fig. 7-6). Now, stop and admire your lovely corners.

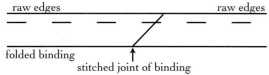

Figure 7-6.

Turn the binding to the back of the quilt and blindstitch it to the backing, just covering the stitching line ⅜" from the edge. Blindstitch the binding all the way to the adjacent raw edge (Fig. 7-7). Fold the adjacent binding to the back and the corner will miter automatically. Secure with a few extra stitches (Fig. 7-8).

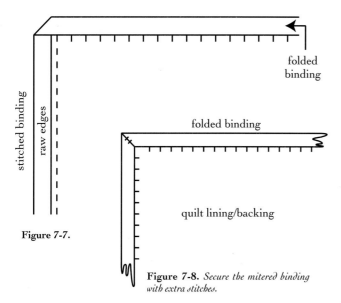

Figure 7-7.

Figure 7-8. *Secure the mitered binding with extra stitches.*

CORDED BINDING

I gave "Kensington Garden" an extra special touch with green cording and magenta binding. (See Plate 19, page 32.) It is detailed, but not difficult. Corded binding is achieved by applying covered commercial cording to the quilt before applying the continuous binding. Purchase ¹⁄₁₆" diameter cording in a fabric shop. Measure the perimeter of your quilt and add an extra 4" per corner (16" total). Preshrink the cording by soaking it in warm water. Then hang it to air dry.

Cut a length plus 4" for each side of the quilt.

Choose a fabric color that has previously been used in the quilt construction for covering the cording. It should either contrast or complement the binding color. To cover the ¹⁄₁₆" cording, cut fabric strips ⅞" wide. This dimension is determined by the following formula:

¹⁄₁₆" cording diameter xz + ⅜" seam allowance x 2 or, ⅛" + ⁶⁄₈" = ⅞" in width.

These strips are cut on the bias. The bias cut results in a neater and tighter covering. There are two methods for cutting continuous bias strips. For the first you will need a square of fabric. Multiply the number of inches needed (perimeter of quilt) by the desired width established previously. Use a calculator to find the square root of that number. That is the size of the fabric square needed.

Cut the square in half diagonally (Fig. 7-9). With the right sides of the fabric facing, join the triangles (Fig. 7-10) using a ¼" seam. Press the seam open. Mark off parallel lines of the predetermined width (Fig. 7-11).

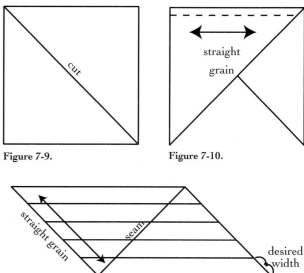

Figure 7-9.

Figure 7-10.

Figure 7-11. *Creating continuous bias strips.*

With right sides together, align the raw straight edges, extending one marked increment beyond the start of line #2 (Fig. 7-12). Sew with a ¼" seam allowance, matching all subsequent marked increments. Cut a continuous strip, starting with the

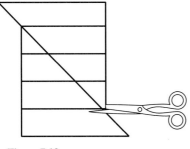

Figure 7-12.

extended end and following the drawn lines on the created tube.

Fold the bias in half lengthwise, wrong sides together, and press. Be careful not to stretch it.

The second method of cutting continuous binding is for people who prefer to use a rotary cutter. Also, at times I cover cording with strips of bias from several coordinated fabrics. Bias strips are cut using this method, then pieced together on the diagonal to make a long length of bias fabrics. This method works well for this purpose.

Align your fabric on a cutting board with a grid and establish the bias (Fig. 7-13).

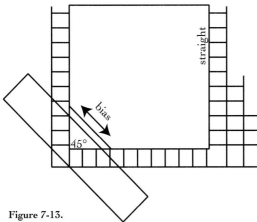

Figure 7-13.

To establish the true bias, align the 45° marker on the ruler along the straight edge of the fabric and vertical grid on the board.

To produce the true bias, the ruler will be on the same number on both the side and the bottom of the grid board (Fig. 7-14).

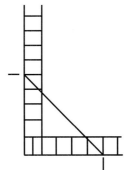

Figure 7-14.

After the first cut, remove and set aside the cut-away triangle of fabric. Fold the remaining fabric as illustrated, lining up the newly cut bias raw edge (Fig. 7-15). It will resemble an envelope.

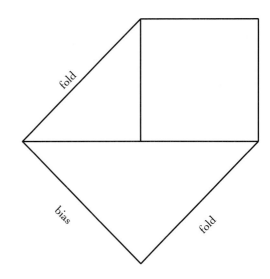

Figure 7-15. *Fold fabric.*

This procedure will allow you to cut increasingly longer bias strips accurately with a 24" see-through ruler and a roller cutter (Fig. 7-16).

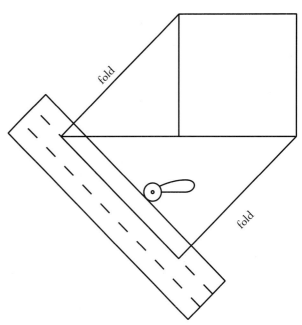

Figure 7-16. *Rotary cutting long bias strips.*

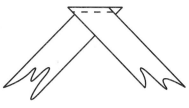

Figure 7-17.

Handle the strips with care. They are true bias strips and will stretch easily. Piece the strips together with a ¼" seam allowance to obtain the required length (Fig. 7-17). Carefully press the seams open.

COVERING THE CORDING

Before it can be applied to the quilt, each piece of the previously cut cording needs to be covered with a length of bias. Cover all four pieces, one for each side of the quilt.

Place the cording down the center (wrong side) of the bias strip and fold the strip over the cord, matching the cut edges.

Using a cording or zipper foot, adjust the needle position, then stitch as close to the cording as possible (Fig. 7-18).

Figure 7-18. *Covering the cording with fabric.*

ATTACHING THE CORDING

Attach the covered cording to the quilt using the cording or zipper foot. Align the raw edges of the bias with the raw edge of quilt, one strip per side.

Begin and end each strip of covered cording with a folded 45° angle, folded it under along the quilt, as illustrated in Figure 7-19.

Note that the *raw edge* of the covered cording's 45° angle must exactly fit the quilt corner (Fig. 7-20).

To begin stitching, insert the machine needle in the folded angle at the position marked x on Figure 7-21. Take a stitch or two forward and back, then continue to apply the covered cording to the quilt on top of the previous stitching. As you approach the next corner, carefully make a 45° fold just in the right place so the angled fold fits the corner precisely. Stitch over the fold, backstitch, and remove the needle from the quilt. Remove the quilt from under the needle and cut the threads. Begin the second side of the cording application and continue until all four sides are completed.

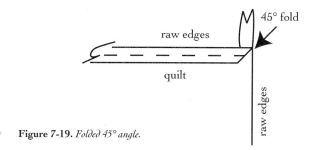

Figure 7-19. *Folded 45° angle.*

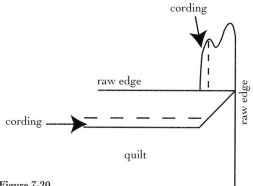

Figure 7-20.

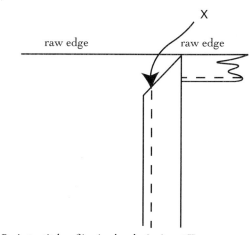

Figure 7-21. *Begin to stitch cording in place beginning at X.*

ADDING THE BINDING

With the cording in place, stitch the binding, as described earlier in the chapter, using the cording or zipper foot. Make sure the stitching cannot be seen when the binding is folded back. Continue to apply continuous binding as in the previous illustrations (Fig. 7-22).

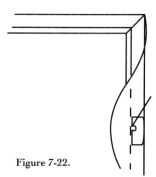

Figure 7-22.

SLEEVE WITH A TUCK

A quilt needs a sleeve if it is to be displayed on the wall at home or at shows. Attaching a sleeve on the back of your masterpiece will make that a reality. The traditional sleeve, where the board or dowel rod is passed through, leaves a bulge on the front of the quilt. A sleeve with a tuck gives extra room for the rod and keeps the face of the quilt flat. Don't let this lengthy set of directions deter you! A sleeve with a tuck is very simple. It's just the directions that appear tedious.

To make a finished size 6" sleeve (required by most exhibitions), cut self-backing fabric 13½" by the width of the quilt, less 2". Fold the fabric in half, right sides together lengthwise, and stitch the cut edges with a ¼" seam allowance. Leave a 3" opening to turn right side out (Fig. 7-23). Turn, and press well.

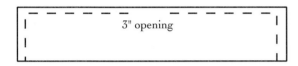

Figure 7-23. *Making a finished sleeve.*

Turn the folded edge of the sleeve back on itself ⅜". Press well. This is the side of the sleeve that will go against the quilt back (Fig. 7-24).

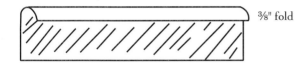

Figure 7-24.

Center the sleeve on the quilt back with the fold parallel to and 1" below the top edge of the quilt (Fig. 7-25).

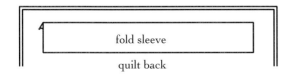

Figure 7-25. *Placing the sleeve behind the quilt.*

Flip the sleeve up and open above the quilt edge (Fig. 7-26).

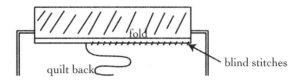

Figure 7-26.

By hand blindstitch along the edge of the sleeve with small stitches through the backing and batting only.

Fold the sleeve back down in place. Blindstitch the lower edge of the sleeve to the quilt back and batting (Fig. 7-27).

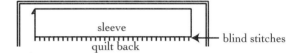

Figure 7-27.

THE LABEL

If you inherited a quilt, particularly an antique quilt, what information would you appreciate being included on the label? Following are some considerations:

Maker's name, of course.

Address (place of residence when the quilt was constructed).

Size (whenever you display at a quilt show, this is always good to know).

Working time, lapsed or specific time; for instance; "Une Belle Mademoiselle": working time 10 months, including 538 hours of quilting time.

Recipient of quilt, if a gift and the occasion, such as a wedding.

Include some historical facts, either on your label or on an accompanying journal. This could be facts about what is going on in the country or personal notes.

One of my quilts includes the information that I worked on the quilt while caring for my daughter, who had been injured in an automobile accident. Another, worked on during my son's baseball games, gives his batting average at the time. How about the weather? Was it particularly hot, cold, icy, or snowy?

Tree of Life

*I*ntrigued by the old Indian palamapores — cotton prints woven in India — I wanted to construct a Tree of Life quilt that would closely resemble the eighteenth-century counterpane at the Shelburne Museum, which I love. Unable to find a chintz fabric printed as such, I selected a chintz with woody vines and a meandering design that included magnificent flowers and leaves. I carefully cut and spliced, overlapped, and manipulated, forming, at long last, a tree. To get the thickness of the tree trunk I wanted to achieve, I found the longest, straightest run of vine, plus the repeat farther along in the fabric, and overlapped the two. This gave me a substantial trunk from which to branch (Plate 24).

Once again I selected portions of the vine to form the branches. Where I needed to splice in a branch, I found a flower or leaf to place over the seam line, as often as possible. This planning took about one month. I pinned the background to a wallboard and then temporarily mounted the trunk and branches until I was comfortable with the effect. I selected the larger flowers to place on the lower branches to keep the visual weight proportional.

To form the hummock, or the hill, where the tree is planted, I selected leaves and portions of large flowers. I carefully chose and cut out sections of a particular flower for petals. From another flower, I got a center. This made me feel very creative. Piece by piece the hummock grew to an appropriate size (Plate 25).

Plate 25.

I centered all of this on a 100% unwashed cotton chintz panel, leaving ample allowance all the way around it until I could select a border fabric. I knew I wanted a smashing, coordinating border reminiscent of the palamapores. From past experience, I realized the repeat and design selection for miter placement would determine the border's ultimate size, and in turn, the size of the center panel. I cut the panel oversized, which allowed me to begin constructing the tree before I made my border selection. As previously explained, my method of appliqué is to execute the blanket stitch in the seam allowance surrounding the cut out motifs. Because cutting portions of flowers, petals, centers,

Plate 24.

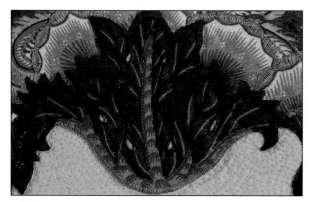

Plate 26. *"Tree of Life," detail.*

dividing leaves, etc., left no background allowance for blanket stitch, I was stymied (Plate 26)!

Just when I thought I'd gotten broderie perse down pat, a new problem reared its ugly head. What should I do? My previous motifs were appliquéd with thread matching the background fabric, and the blanket stitch was executed around the edge of the motif. For "Tree of Life" I stitched on the motif with thread matching each one instead of the background fabric. This way the row of knots fell on the raw edge, and the stitches rest on the design. I really enjoyed this, and I was satisfied with the appearance.

But I couldn't stop with just the perimeter stitching. I began to embellish with DMC machine embroidery thread inside each motif. I used chain stitches, outline stitches, blanket stitches, and French knots. What a field day I had (Plate 27)!

Plate 27. *"Tree of Life," detail.*

Finally, I just had to say to myself, "put the needle away. Enough is enough!" The finished work resembles the cutwork my grandmother tried to teach me as a child. She thought she had failed, and I never thought I'd be doing that tedious work! As I appliquéd the tree in place, every trip to the fabric store found me searching for a border fabric, to no avail. As the center portion of the quilt neared completion, the need to secure appropriate border fabric became a major priority.

With "Tree" panels in hand, my friend Rose and I took over the drapery department of a favorite fabric store. We considered a variety of possibilities, draping each one around the "Tree" panel, which was now mounted on bolts of fabric. Other shoppers readily offered advice, but the final choice was Rose's. She selected an opulent paisley that reflected the design of the tree as well as its predominant colors. Little did we realize just how troublesome the paisley print would be to miter (Plate 28).

Plate 28. *"Tree of Life," detail.*

The paisley's configuration prevented placing a miter through the center of the design elements to form a mirror image on the border's corners. For two months I worked the material. I was never completely satisfied. Finally, I set a time limit for myself. Within a day I would have my "Tree of Life" miters done. I am pleased with the results. Almost all of the paisley conformations worked together (Plate 29, page 56).

Now, I just had to fit my tree panel into the frame. I did this by marking the centers of the top, bottom, and sides of both the panel and border fabric frame. Working from the centers outward toward the corners and using a walking foot, I accomplished my mission (Fig. 8-1, page 56). I developed scrolls of feathers, using a dime for a smooth, uniform frond. They fit nicely around the tree, gracefully adding interest to it (Fig. 8-2, page 57).

I quilted the border along both the narrow inner and outer edge of the fabric following the design. Between these two perimeters I did crosshatch quilting.

Plate 29. *"Tree of Life," detail.*

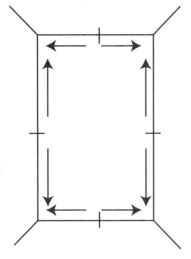

Figure 8-1. *Marking the top, bottom, and sides of the panels and border fabric.*

I made the lines close together, carrying through with the theory that all areas of the quilt should be uniformly quilted. Since the area around the tree was very intensely quilted, then the border needed to be. Visually, close quilting is attractive to the eye; in reality, heavy quilting in one area tends to pucker the fabric. To make a piece lay flat and hang straight, a lot of quilting is needed over the entire surface.

The label I prepared reads:

> Tree of Life
> 63" x 55.5"
> Appliqué: 412 hours
> Quilting: 683.5 hours
> over a period of 3 years
> 524 stuffed feathers
> Barbara W. Barber
> 34 Langworthy Road
> Westerly, RI 02891

Plate 30. *"Tree of Life," detail.*

THE GIFT OF FULFILLMENT

As I work on my quilts, I am complete;
having a needle in my hand makes me whole.
God has given me a gift; and as I use it,
fulfillment comes. It's that simple!

"Whatever thy hand findest to do,
do it with all of thy might." Eccl. 9:10.

Quilting design
for "Tree of Life."

Center bottom,
reversed and
overlapped.

Figure 8-2.

Used three times
each side of tree,
sometimes reversed.

Figure 8-3.

Quilting design
for "Tree of Life."

Quilting design
for "Tree of Life."

Center top design.

Figure 8-4.

Feathers designed and placed
around tree to add visual interest
to an otherwise empty area.

overlap A

Quilting design
for "Tree of Life."

Figure 8-5.

Quilting design
for "Tree of Life."

overlap A

Figure 8-6.

Original designed for center bottom.
Fold on marked line to achieve mirror image.

Quilting design
for "Tree of Life."

fold

Figure 8-7.

Bibliography

Elly Sienkiewicz. *Quilter's Newsletter Magazine*. No. 273, June 1995

.Orlofsky, Myron and Patsy. *Quilts in America*. New York, New York: McGraw-Hill, 1974.

Bullard, Lacy Folmar and Betty Jo Shiell. *Chintz Quilts: Unfading Glory*. Tallahassee, Florida: Serendipity Publishers, 1983.

Nadelstern, Paula, and Lynnell Hancock. *Quilting Together*. New York, New York: Crown Publishers Inc., 1988.

Beyer, Jinny. *Patchwork Patterns*. McLean, Virginia: EPM Publications, Inc., 1979.

Information Supplied by:
Shelburne Museum, Shelburne, VT 05482

About the Author

Barbara W. Barber is a mother of six, grandmother of eight, an avid quilter, and a short-order cook. Her quilts range from the very elegant broderie perse to tongue-in-cheek, comical, spiritual, photo-transfer, strip-pieced, and "Wonder-Under" quickies.

HOPE was the Rhode Island winning entry for the Great American Quilt Festival, sponsored by the Museum of American Folk Art and the 3-M Company, held in New York City, 1986, recognizing the Statue of Liberty's 100th anniversary. Her quilt CONNECTING THREADS was also the successful Rhode Island entry for a similar program held three years later. Both quilts were displayed nationally and internationally for a three year period following the main show.

She co-founded the Ninigret Quilters, a continuing local club. Barbara is a member of numerous quilt organizations, including the American Quilter's Society, the Eastcoast Quilters Alliance, the New England Quilt Guild, and the New England Quilt Museum. She is active in the Ninigret, Narragansett Bay, and Thames River Quilt clubs.

In addition to designing and making quilts, she lectures and teaches quilting workshops on a rather extensive basis, and has hosted a quilter's retreat at the Alton Jones campus of the University of Rhode Island for the past 12 years. Barbara was instrumental in initiating, and served as a key voluntary consultant for the university's recent antique quilt search and documentation project, a work that is soon to be published. She has also served as a quilting instructor in the Rhode Island Arts Counsel Apprentice Program.

Quoting the artist: "Quilting is for me, as it is for many others, therapy. I have often realized how rewarding it can be while raising children. In fifteen minutes I can successfully piece a quilt block, but it is possible to be fifteen years into the child raising program before realizing positive feedback. It is no wonder so many moms are avid quilters with that kind of rapid gratification."

AQS Books on Quilts

This is only a partial listing of the books on quilts that are available from the American Quilter's Society. AQS books are known the world over for their timely topics, clear writing, beautiful color photographs, and accurate illustrations and patterns. Most of the following books are available from your local bookseller, quilt shop, or public library. If you are unable to locate certain titles in your area, you may order by mail from the AMERICAN QUILTER'S SOCIETY, P.O. Box 3290, Paducah, KY 42002-3290. Customers with Visa or MasterCard may phone in orders from 7:00–4:00 CST, Monday–Friday, Toll Free 1-800-626-5420. Add $2.00 for postage for the first book ordered and $0.40 for each additional book. Include item number, title, and price when ordering. Allow 14 to 21 days for delivery.